AF333882

CYLINDERS

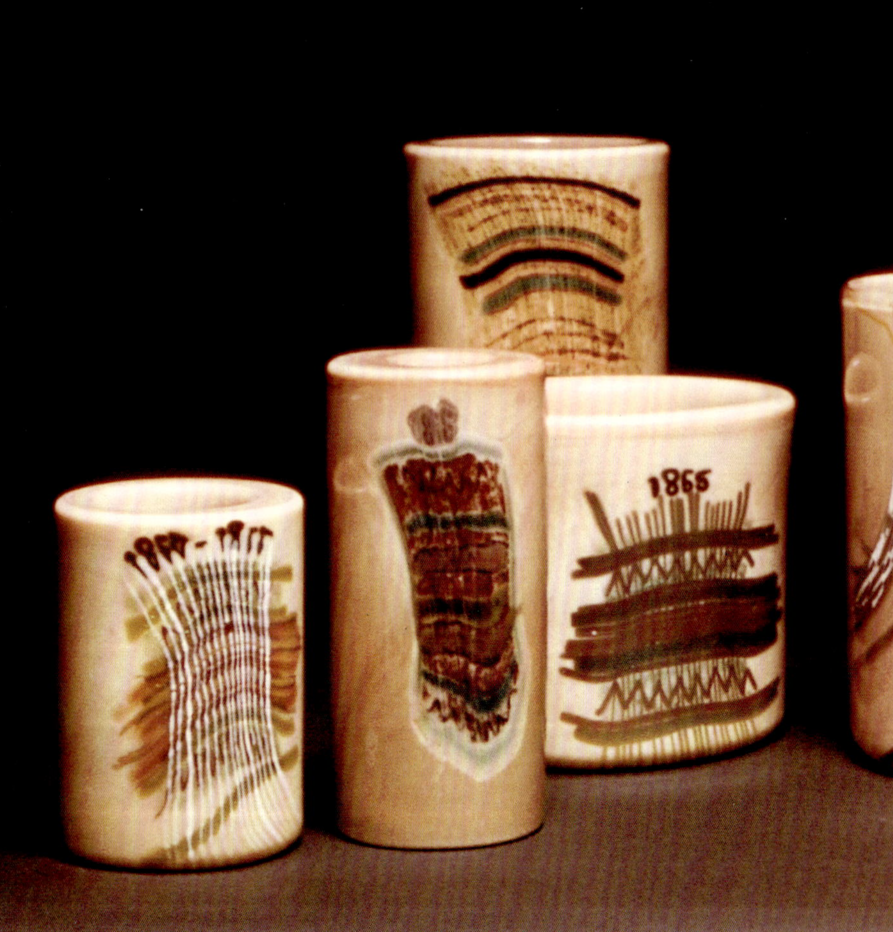

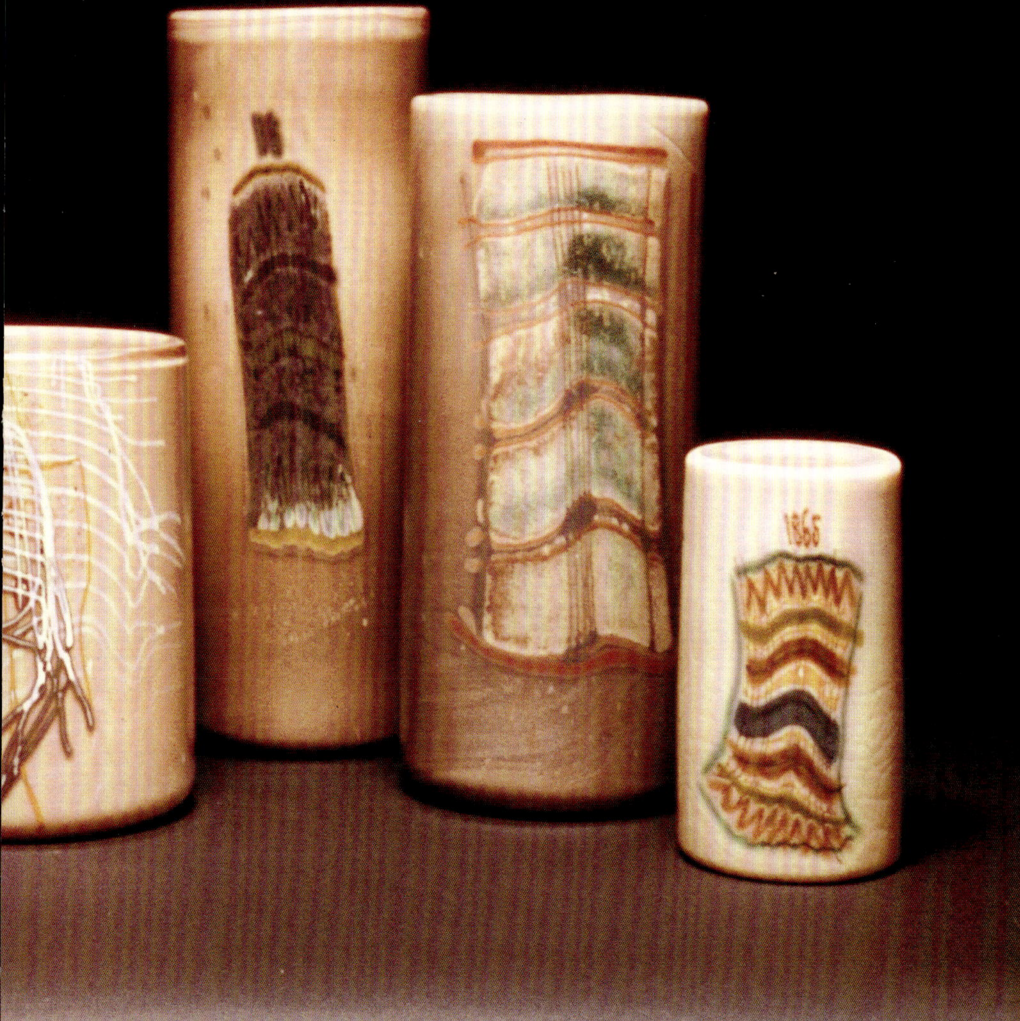

CYLINDERS AND *SOFT CYLINDERS*: CHIHULY'S CANVASES

ONE OF THE MOST CRITICAL DISCOURSES OF LATE-TWENTIETH-CENTURY ART involved the reevaluation of all the visual arts. Traditional hierarchies were overthrown as artists from a multitude of backgrounds expanded the definition of fine art into areas of advertisement, design, function, surface decoration, and commercial art. Dale Chihuly was a pivotal figure in this dialogue, over the years addressing primarily the blurring of boundaries separating sculpture, design, and decorative arts. However, in his multiyear *Cylinders* and *Soft Cylinders* series, Chihuly has used the vessel to extend this discussion into painting as well.

While artists in all media have used the vessel form as a three-dimensional canvas, Chihuly's approach has been revolutionary: form and decoration literally become one. The "pickup" drawing technique that Chihuly developed in 1974 at Pilchuck Glass School in Washington State, with the assistance of friends and colleagues Italo Scanga and James Carpenter, several students, and a National Endowment for the Arts grant, involves pulling glass threads from glass rods, laying them out, and heating them to form a motif. Placed upon a smooth flat surface, this element is fused onto a rolling gob of hot glass. The result is an image fully integrated into the form rather than laid or inlaid onto it—a dramatic concept not just within the history of glass.

By 2000, most of the technical issues in fusing preformed three-dimensional glass elements onto the *Cylinders*

Preceding page:
Navajo Blanket
Cylinders

1975

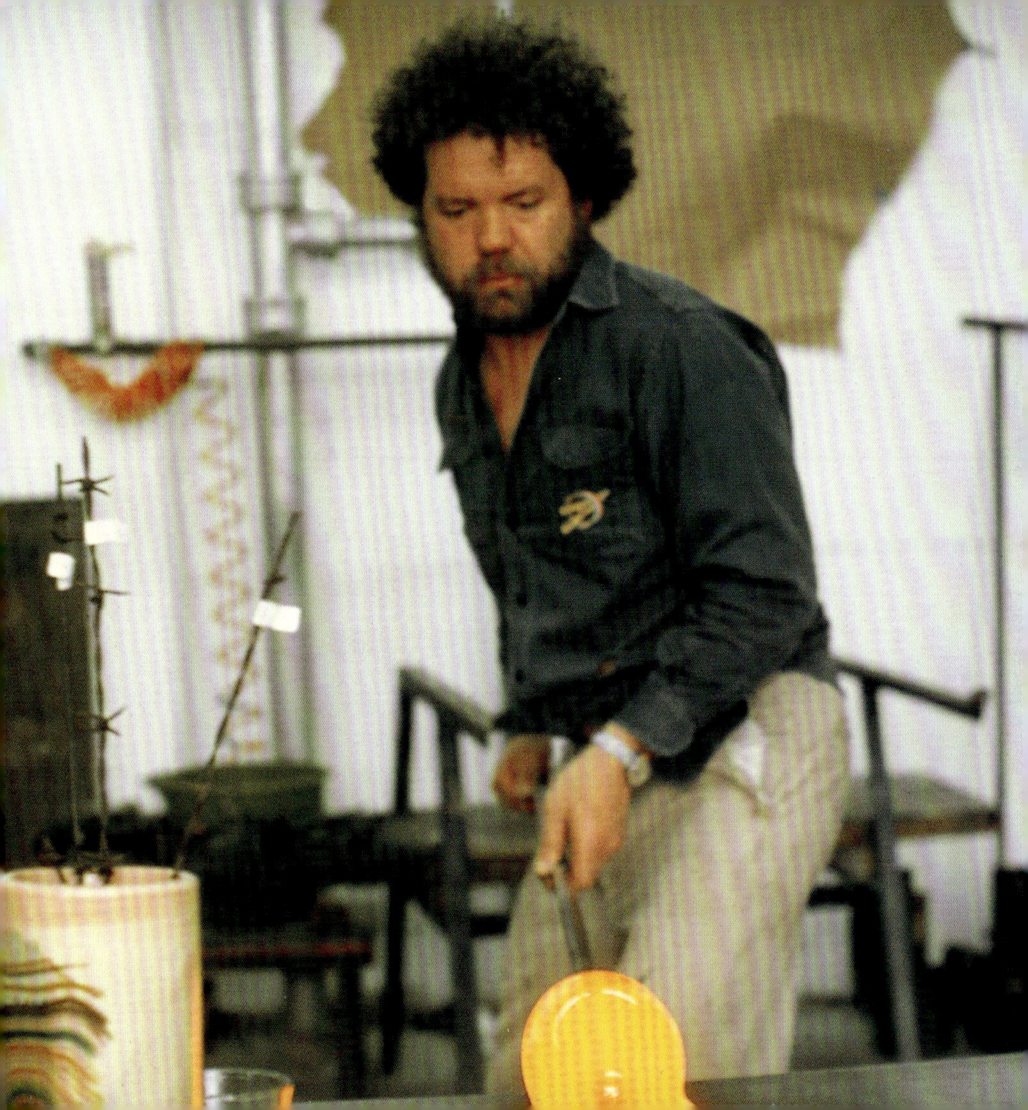

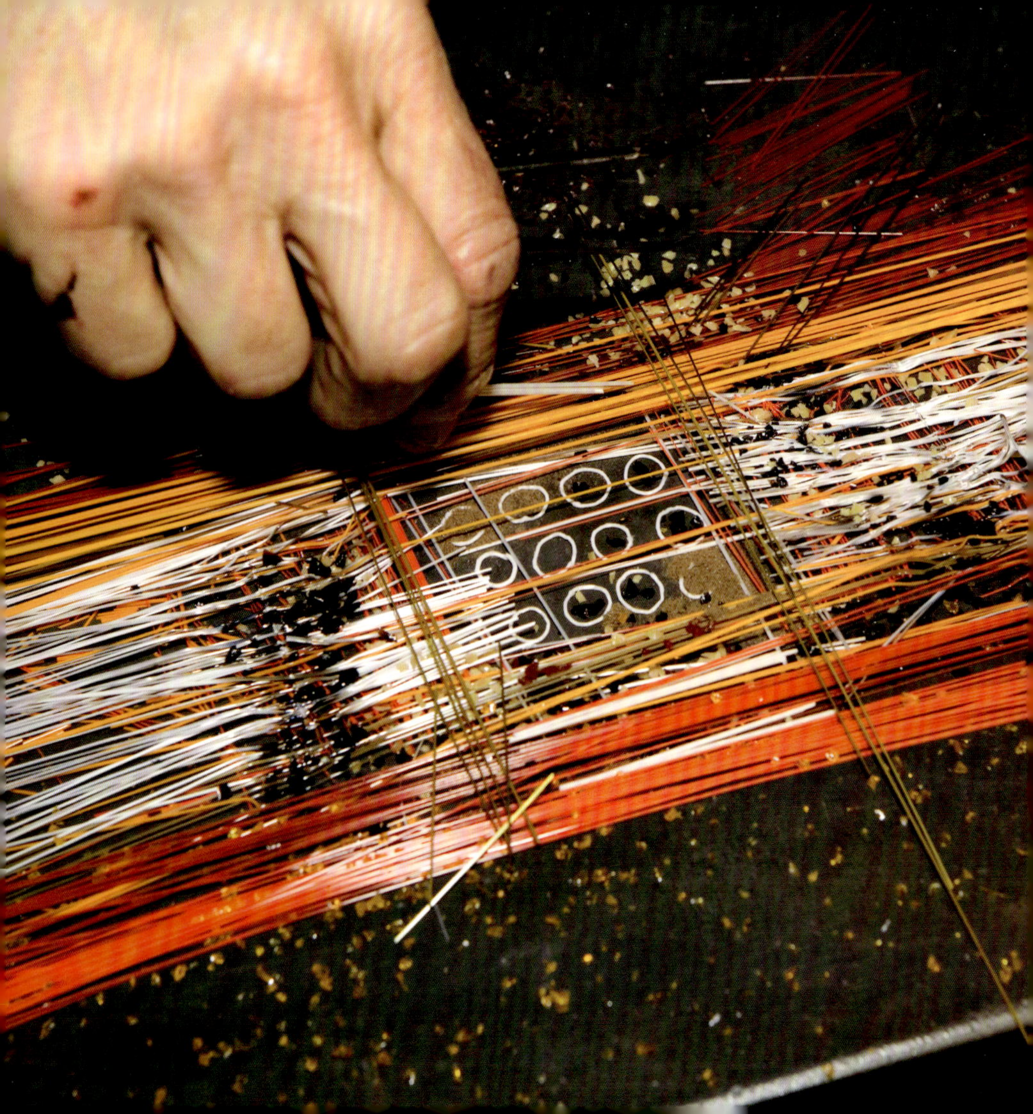

were resolved. In the 1999 *Jerusalem Cylinders*, sharp-edged crystals, reminiscent of Jerusalem stone, are fused onto transparent, subtly colored cylindrical and conical forms that are either crackled or decorated with frit or bubbles. These works and the subsequent *Putti + Sealife* (2000) challenge the boundaries between painting and sculpture in ways similar to the shaped canvases of contemporaries such as Elizabeth Murray.

The pickup drawing technique, which is a paradigm for the collaboration that has marked Chihuly's career, was developed prior to the life-changing automobile accident in 1976 that damaged Chihuly's vision and left him unable to blow glass on his own. Carpenter is said to have been the first to have attempted the technique; Kate Elliott, who met Chihuly at Pilchuck in 1974 and subsequently served as his assistant at the Rhode Island School of Design, was responsible for the initial thread drawings for the 1975 *Floodline* and earliest *Navajo Blanket Cylinders*. Flora Mace, whom Chihuly convinced in the summer of 1975 to learn the technique, soon excelled in complex, abstract patterns as well as realistic imagery. Mace, in fact, first developed the means to feature words on the *Irish Cylinders*, addressing contemporary larger concerns regarding the written word as image. Joey Kirkpatrick joined the

Chihuly/Mace team in 1979, assuming responsibility for setting Mace's designs on the heated steel table for pickup. Now Chihuly continues to call upon Mace and Kirkpatrick to execute all drawings.

The vessels themselves play a critical role in experiencing these drawings. Blown first by Chihuly and later by Benjamin Moore, the earliest *Cylinders*, dating from 1974 through the end of 1975, include the legendary *Navajo Blanket Cylinder* series, executed in Peachblow glass with its characteristic pink/pinkish-yellow hue that reminded Chihuly of the Southwest, and the *Irish Cylinders* series, largely blown from a more transparent greenish glass used in Humpen, Northern European sixteenth- to eighteenth-century beakers. Because Peachblow glass is difficult to blow, these early forms were small, but they had the thick rigid walls necessary for the pickup drawings. Imagery determined their frontal orientation.

The "themes" of the *Cylinders* have come from various sources or circumstances. The *Jerusalem Cylinders*, for example, were created to commemorate the large-scale installation *Chihuly in the Light of Jerusalem 2000*; similarly, the *Irish Cylinders* (with images from James Joyce) were created for use during a lecture trip to England and Ireland. However, the majority of the *Cylinders* and *Soft*

Navajo Blanket Cylinders

1974–75

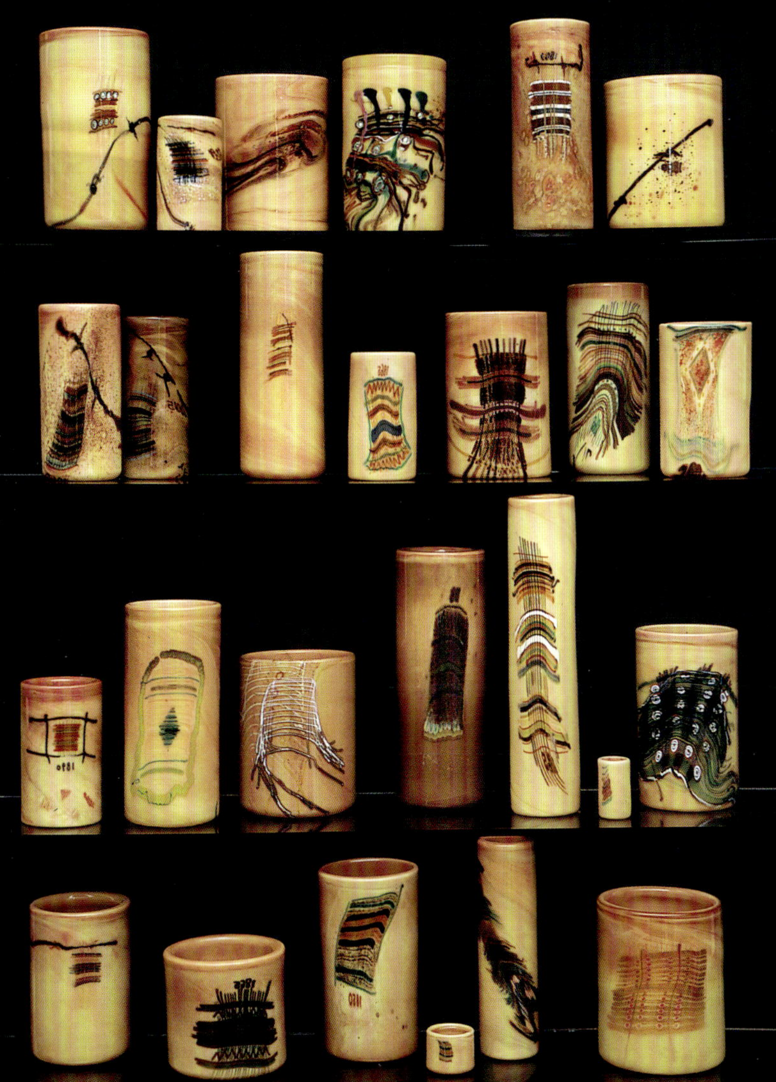

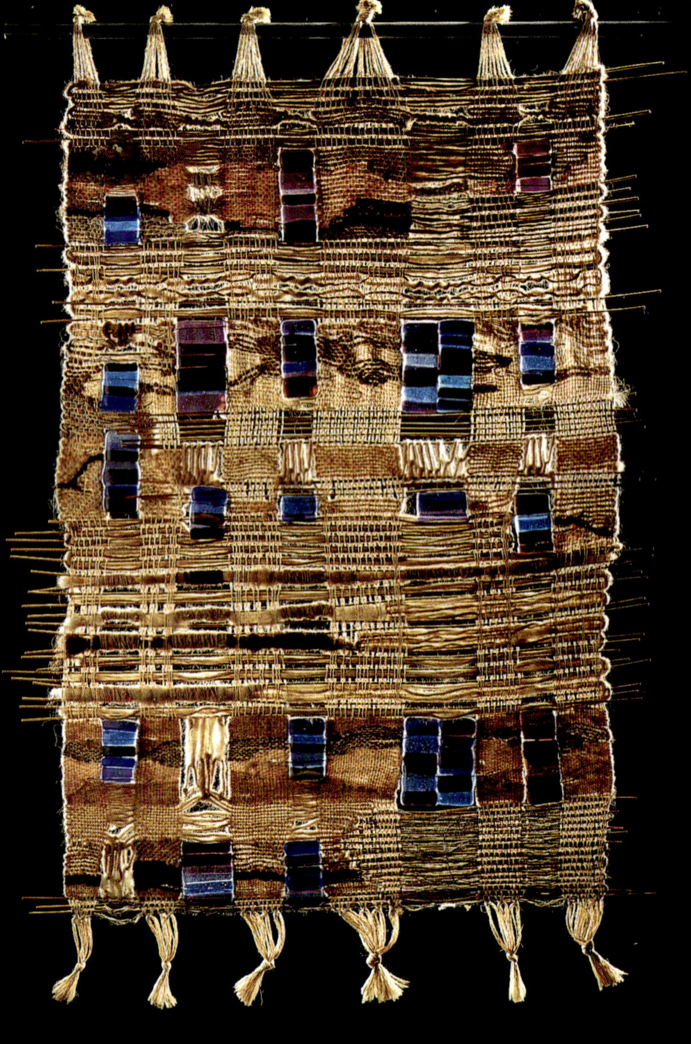

Cylinders demonstrate Chihuly's fascination with weaving and his passion for American Indian trade blankets.

His initial interest in combining glass and textiles was sparked by experiments at the University of Washington in Seattle, from 1960 to 1962 and again from 1963 to 1965, weaving small pieces of glass into tapestries. Exhibitions in the 1970s at the Museum of Art, Rhode Island School of Design, and at the Museum of Fine Arts, Boston, which included Navajo blankets, led Chihuly to collecting. He focused on the more affordable manufactured trade blankets, often called "Pendletons" after the only surviving manufacturer, which were made specifically to exchange for Native American handmade objects. The idea of using the Navajo and Indian trade blankets as motifs for pickup drawings on *Cylinders* grew out of Chihuly's residency in 1974 at Santa Fe's Institute of American Indian Arts: their warp and weft reminded him of the glass threads. Over the years, Chihuly has continued to admire and respond to the colors and dissimilar, double-weave patterns on the front and back of the trade blankets. In fact, the latter may have served as inspiration for other series such as the *Macchia*, in which the interiors differ from the exteriors.

Chihuly has revisited the *Cylinder* series many times since the mid-1970s, using lead gaffers Benjamin Moore,

Weaving with Fused Glass

1965, 33 x 24 x 4"

William Morris, Richard Royal, and James Mongrain. Better-equipped hotshops and increased proficiency in glassblowing have led to refinement of the forms. By 1978, the *Cylinders* created for the Smithsonian Institution's one-person show had become larger and sleeker with thinner walls. Even though the drawings were less complex, the application of thin layers of colored powders led to more diverse areas of color over the entire vessel. In comparison, the *Pilchuck Cylinders*, created six years later, are more exuberant: almost double in size, they are layered with translucent colors and overrun with linear patterns that are reinforced by colorful lip wraps.

This aesthetic culminated in the 1984 *Soft Cylinders*, in which Chihuly's misshapen, sagging *Baskets*, formed by gravity and heat during the blowing process, become the "canvases." The expressionistic shapes of the forms, with their dissimilar exteriors and interiors, interact with complex linear pickup drawings on the exterior. Lip wraps emphasize the horizontality of the designs. In order to create a greater sense of depth between the exterior inner layer of glass and its surface, detailed glass thread drawings are fused onto blown shards and surrounded by hundreds of thick glass threads on a hot plate before being enveloped into the final hot gather of glass. The loose

Pilchuck Cylinders

1984

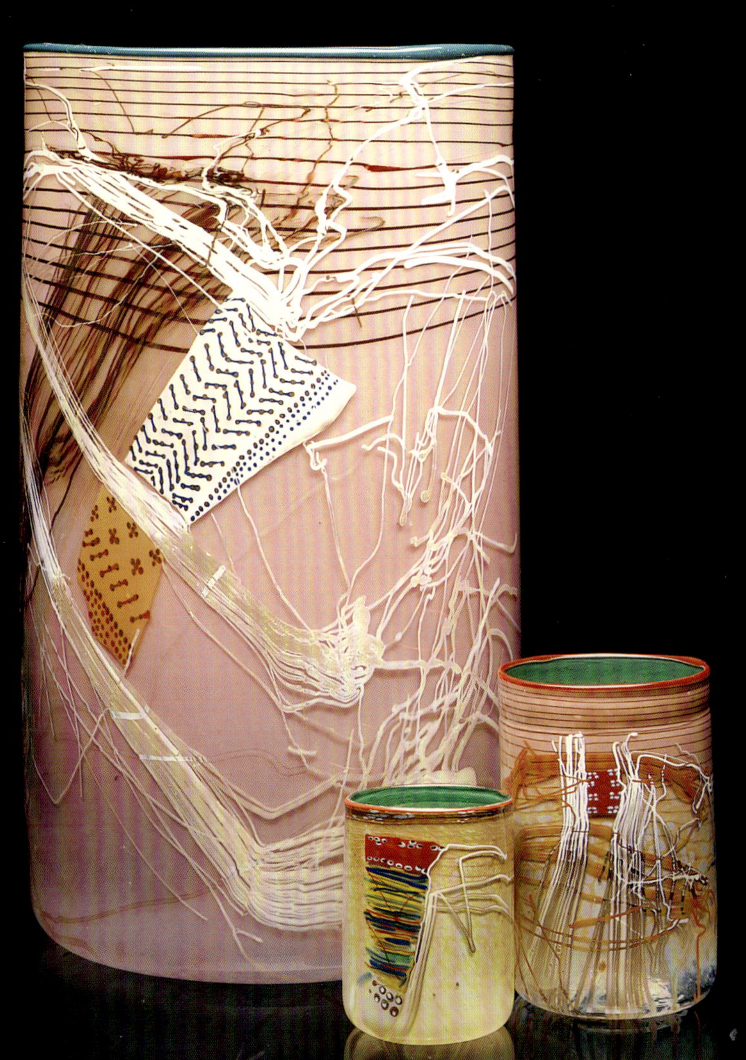

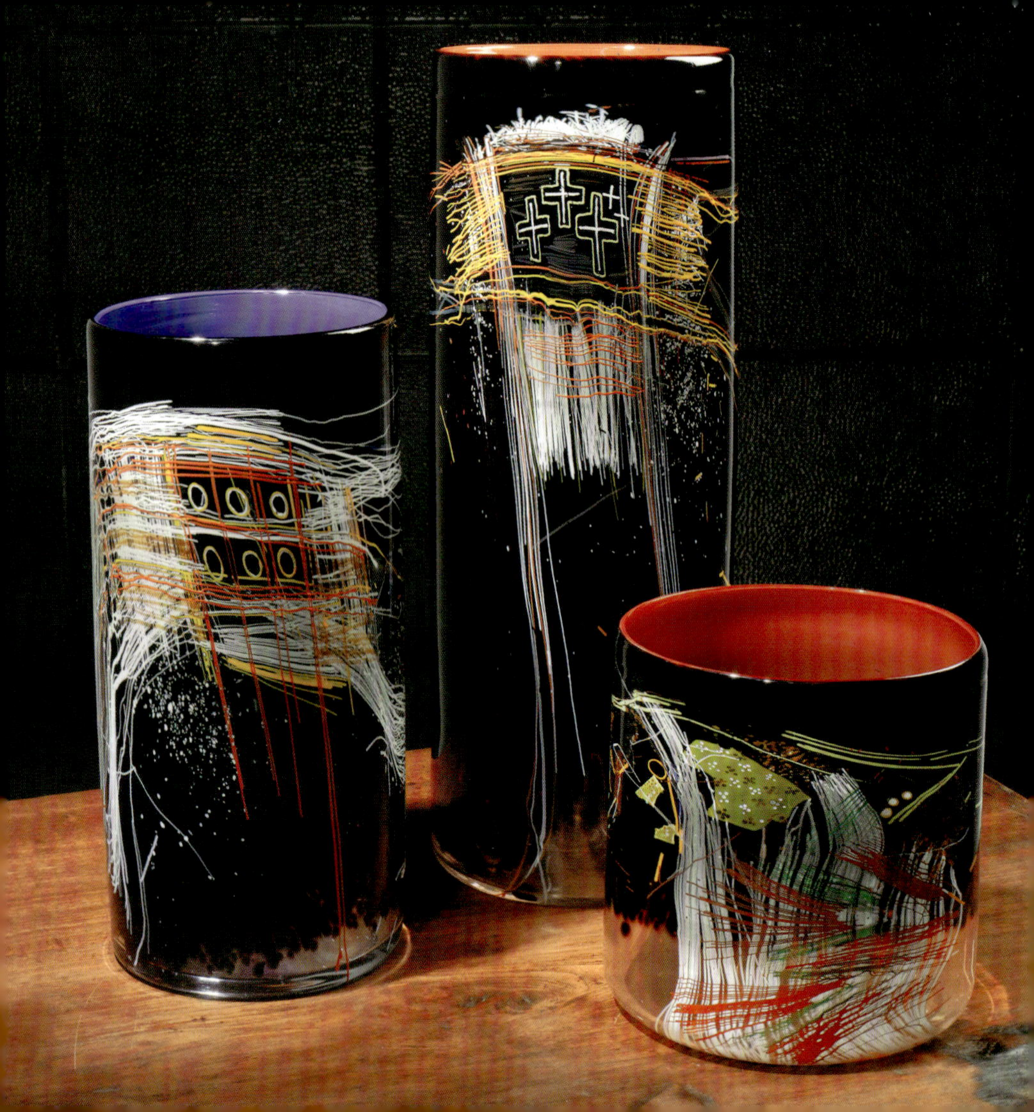

threads provide strong diagonal thrusts into the exterior layers of glass.

Subsequent iterations present mature statements of earlier formulas. For example, while the 1995 *Peachblow Cylinders*, in scale and wall thickness, demonstrate a mastery of this very difficult glass, in the 2006 *Black Cylinders* the artist was able to explore intense color on essentially monumental, volumetric black glass canvases. To heighten the effect, Chihuly specified no lip wrap and solid opaque colors for the interiors, with exterior shard drawings formed over white glass threads. The *Clear Cylinders*, yet another creative restatement, provide the ultimate transparent surface for the interaction of colored threads.

Davira S. Taragin

Former Director of Exhibitions and Programs,

Racine Art Museum;

former Curator, The Detroit Institute of Arts,

Toledo Museum of Art

Black Cylinders

2006

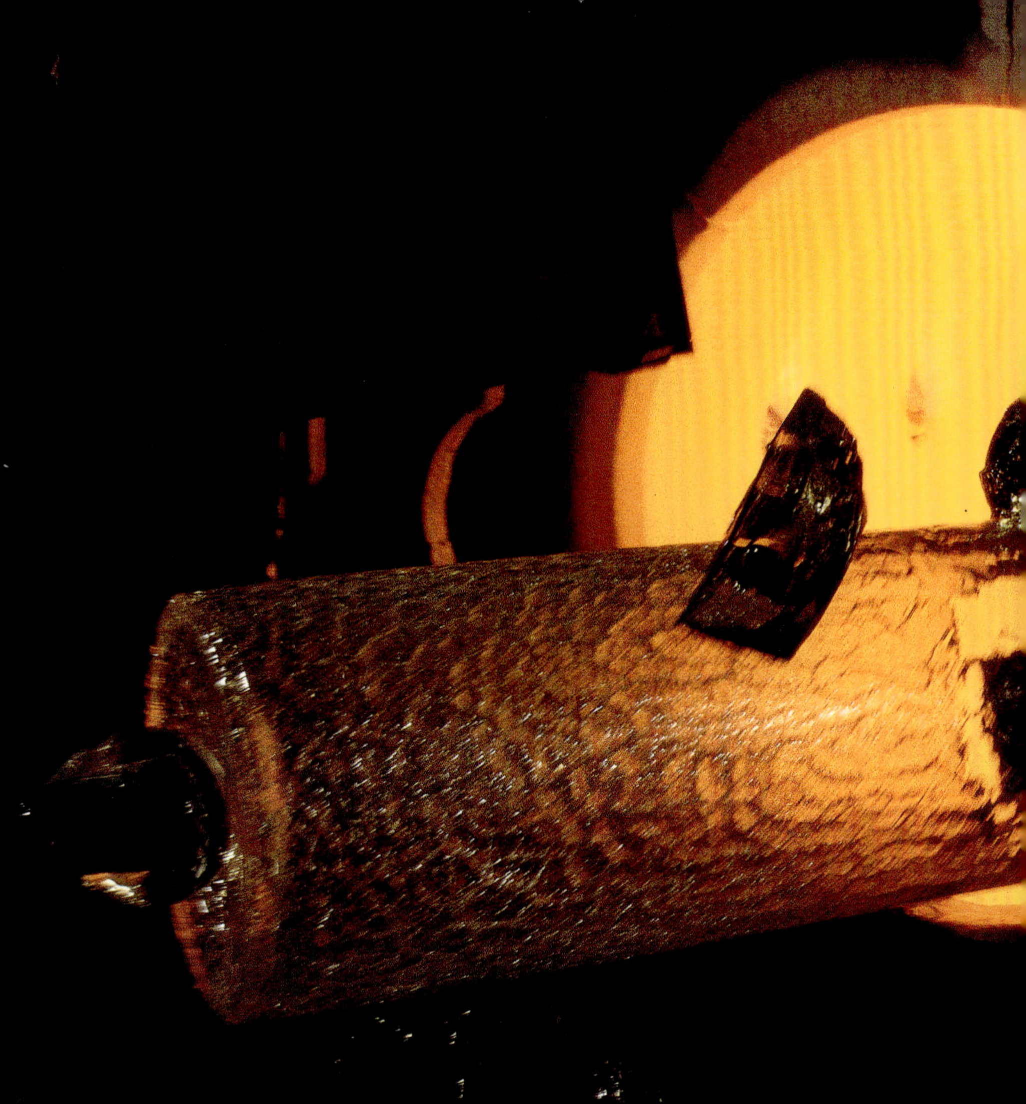

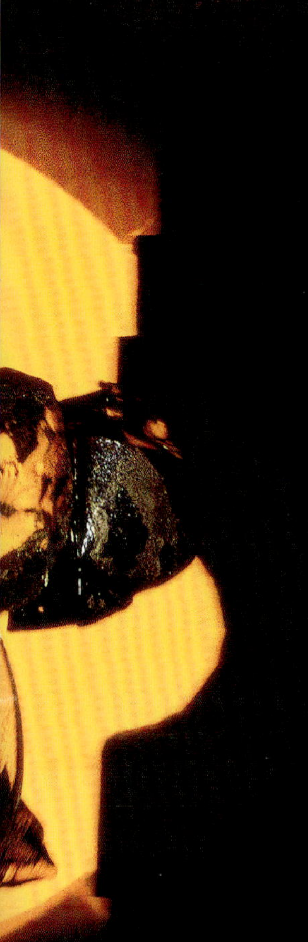

Navajo Blanket
Cylinders

1975

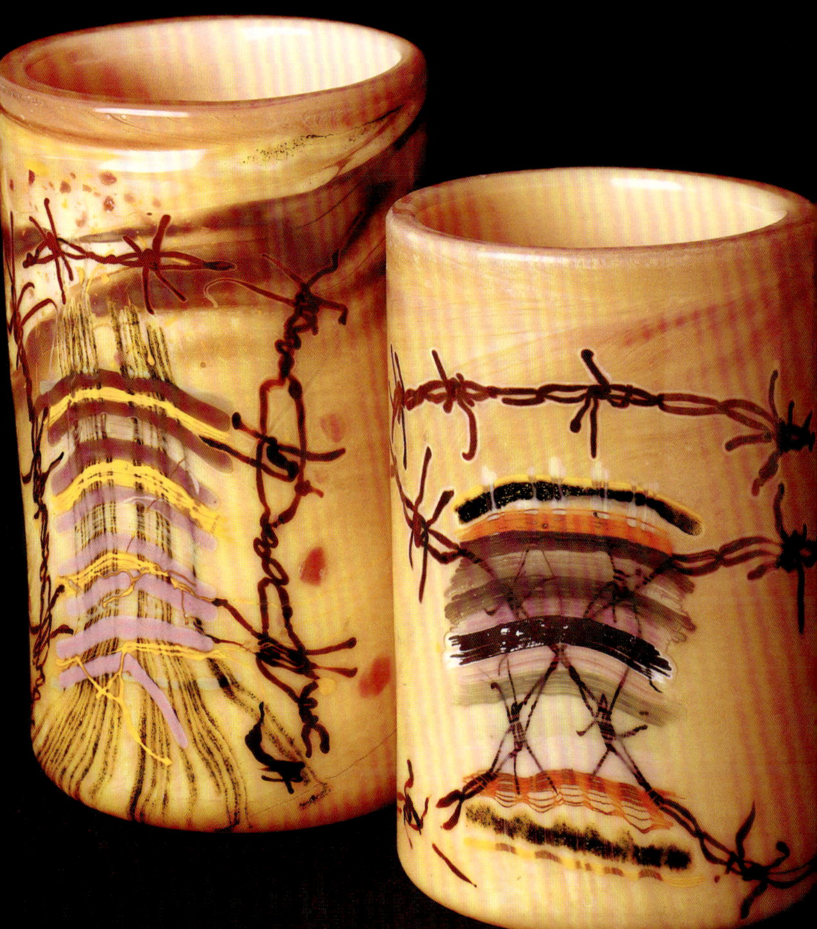

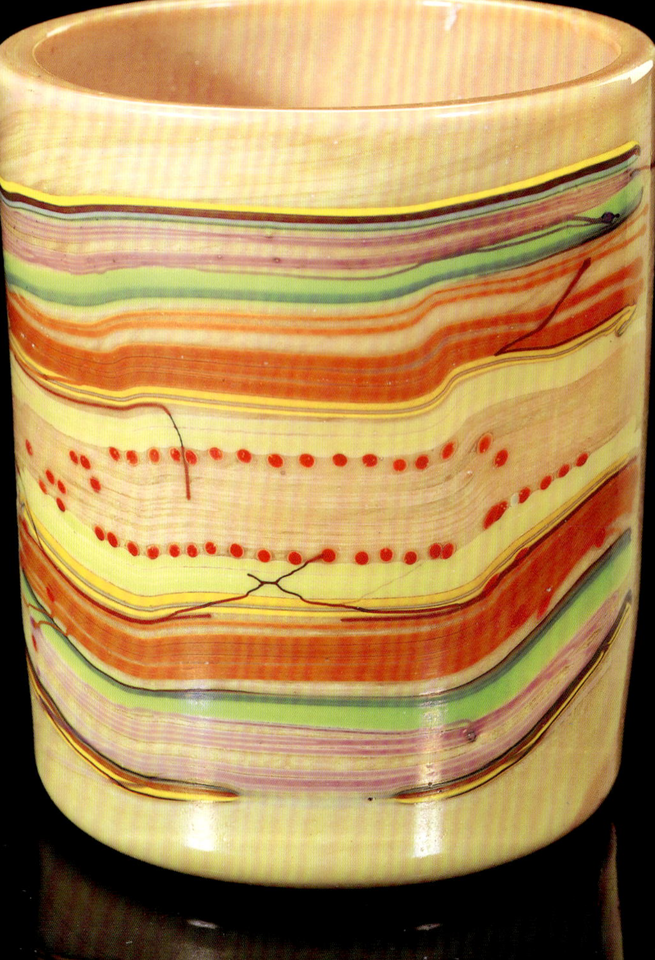

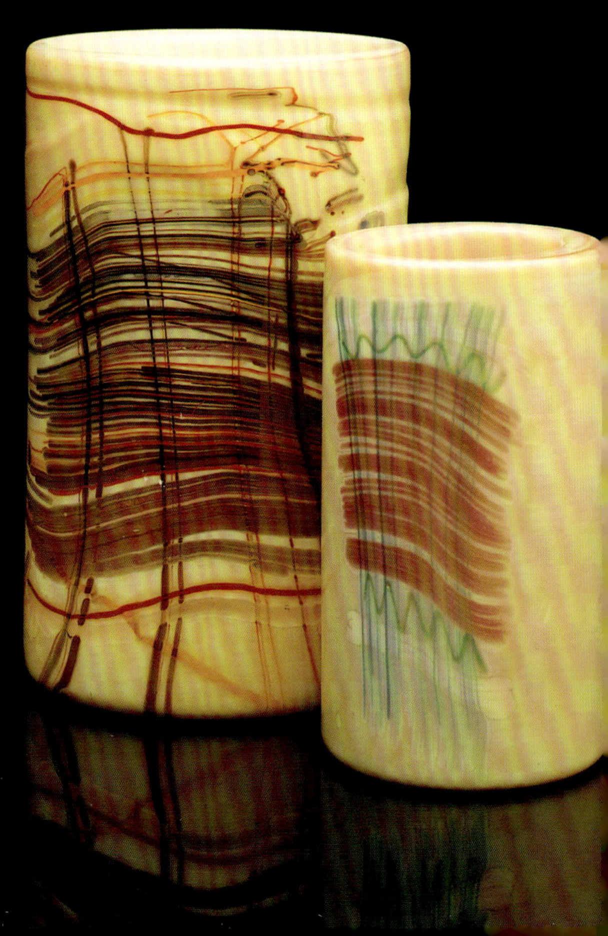

**Full Wrap
Pueblo Cylinder**

1975, 10 x 8 x 8"

**Navajo Blanket
Cylinders**

1975

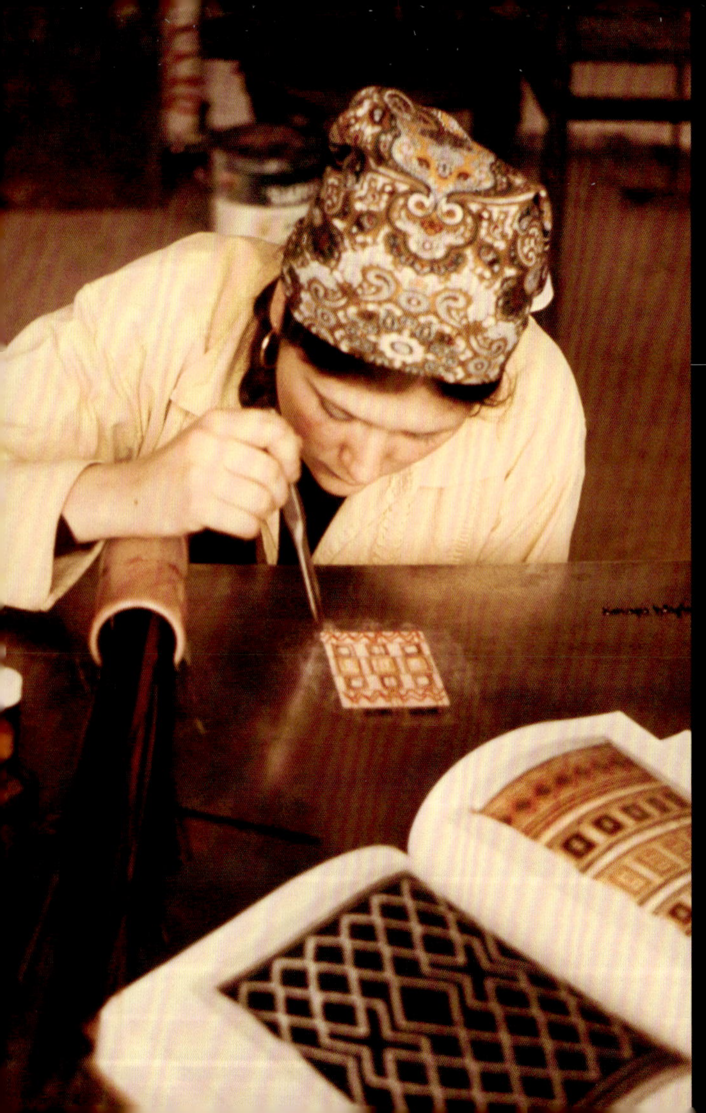

Kate Elliott

Rhode Island School of Design
Providence, Rhode Island, 1975

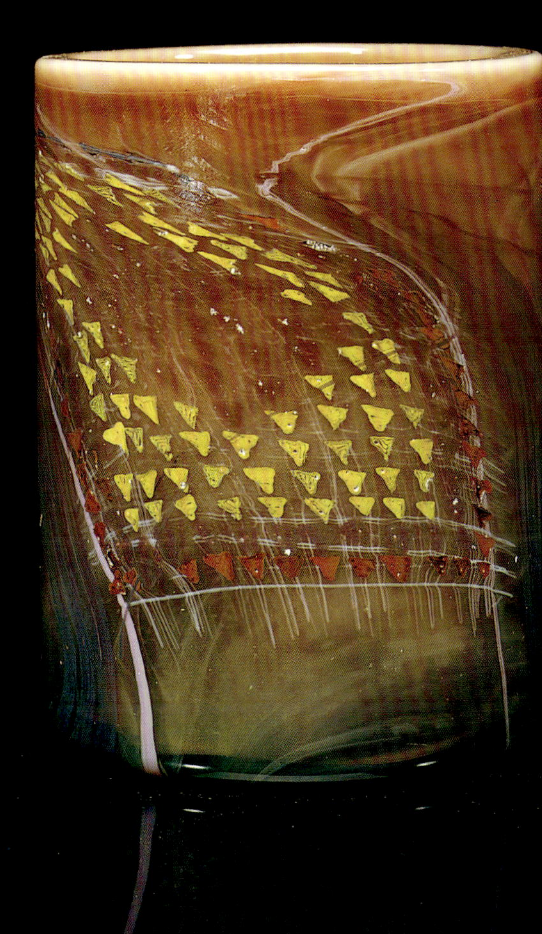

Blanket Cylinder

1990, 9 x 7 x 7"

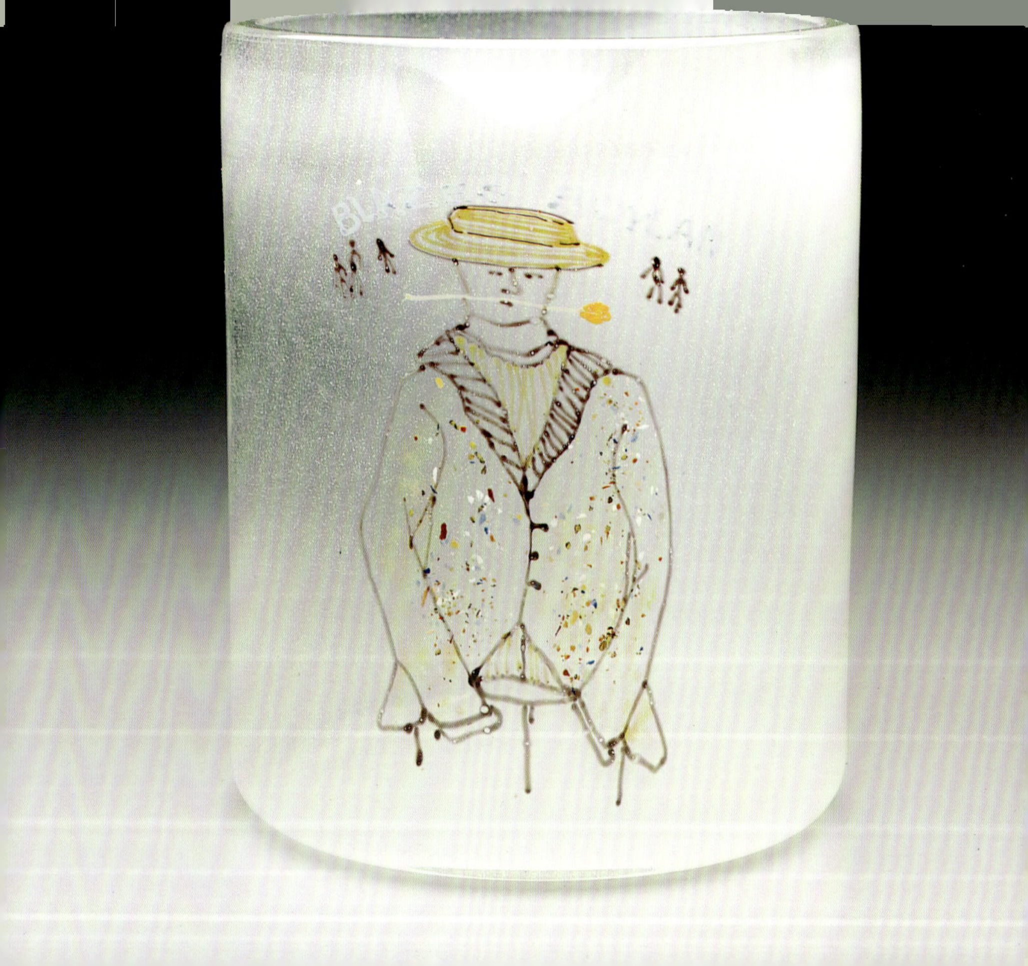

Irish Cylinder #38

In collaboration
with Seaver Leslie
1975, 10 x 8 x 8"

Irish Cylinders

In collaboration
with Seaver Leslie
1975

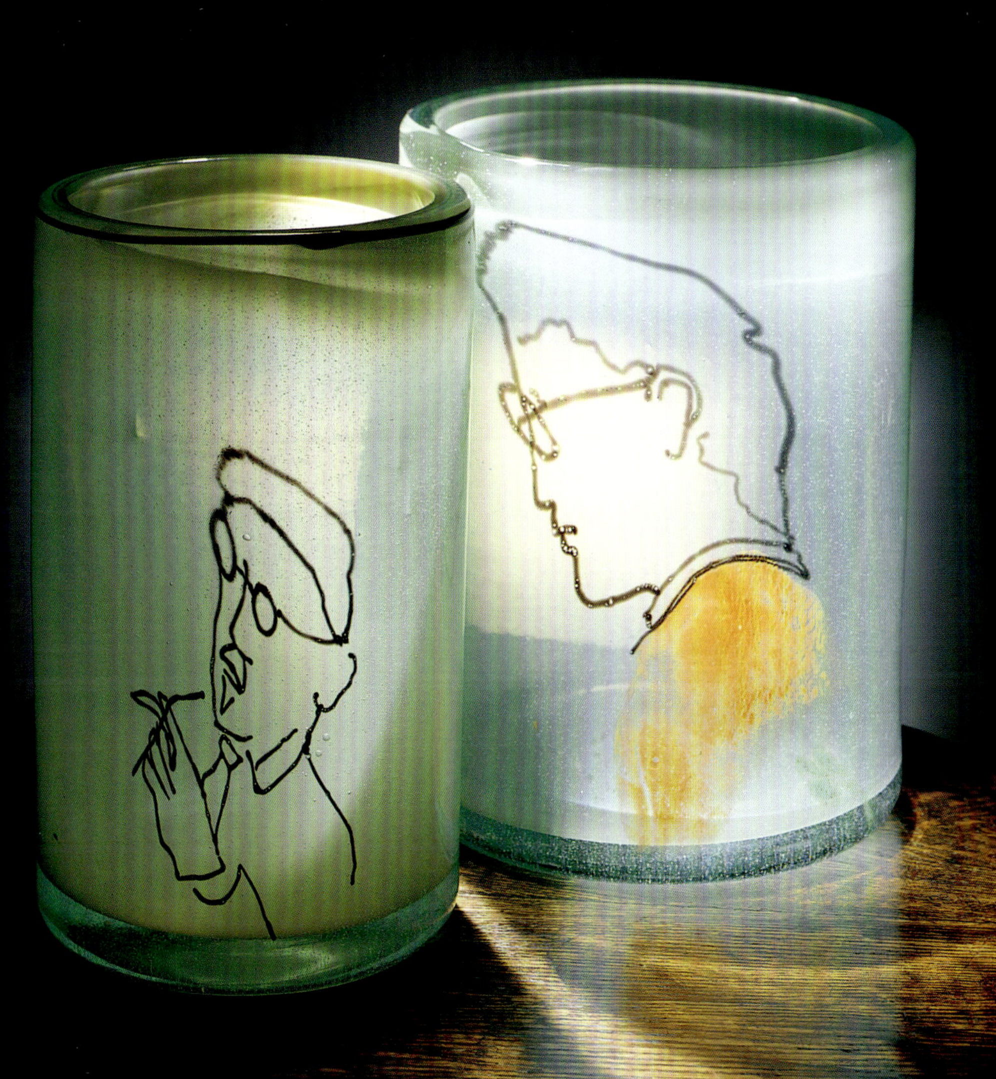

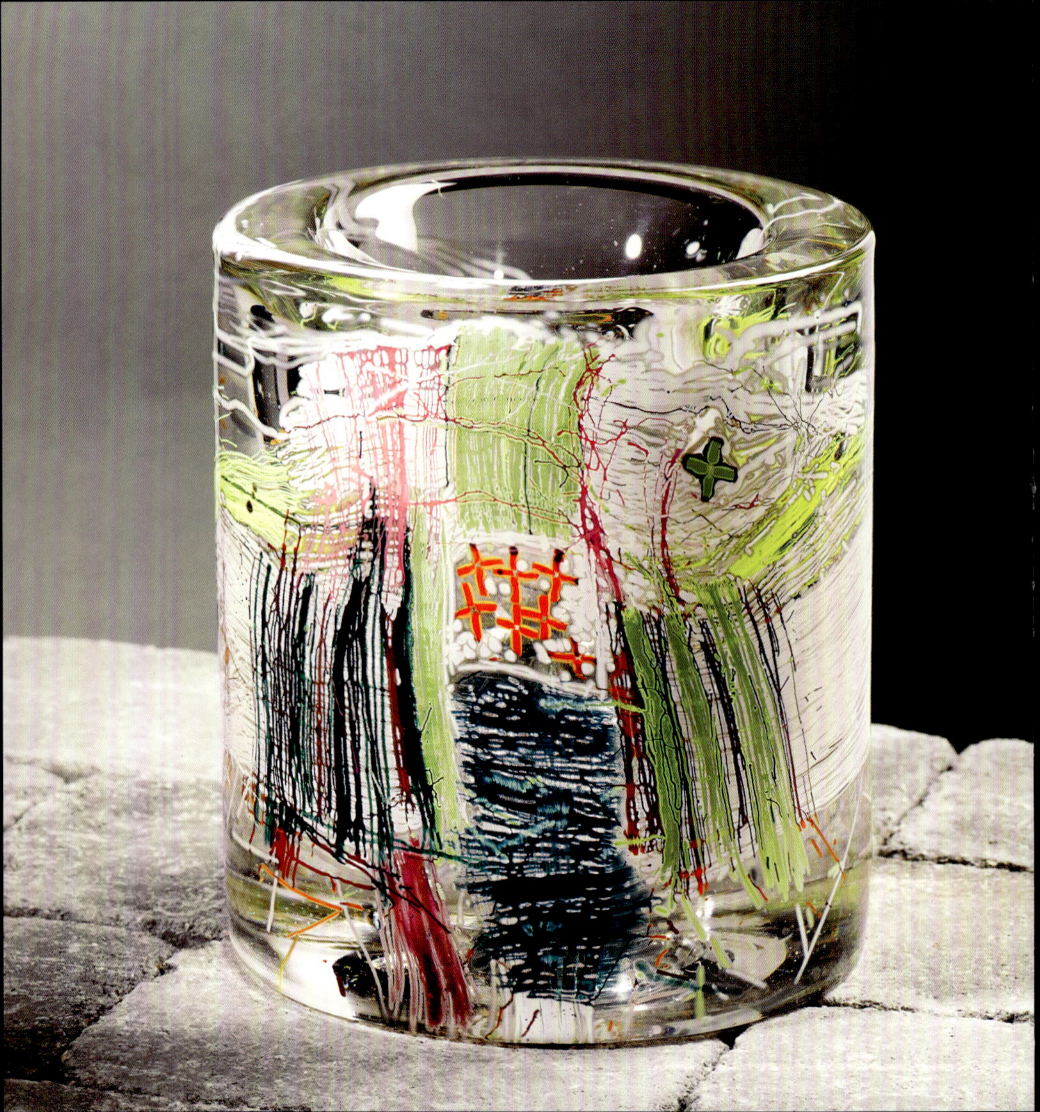

Clear Cylinder #10

2006, 11 x 10 x 10"

**Old Copper and Ruby
Cylinder Drawing**

2009, 30 x 22"

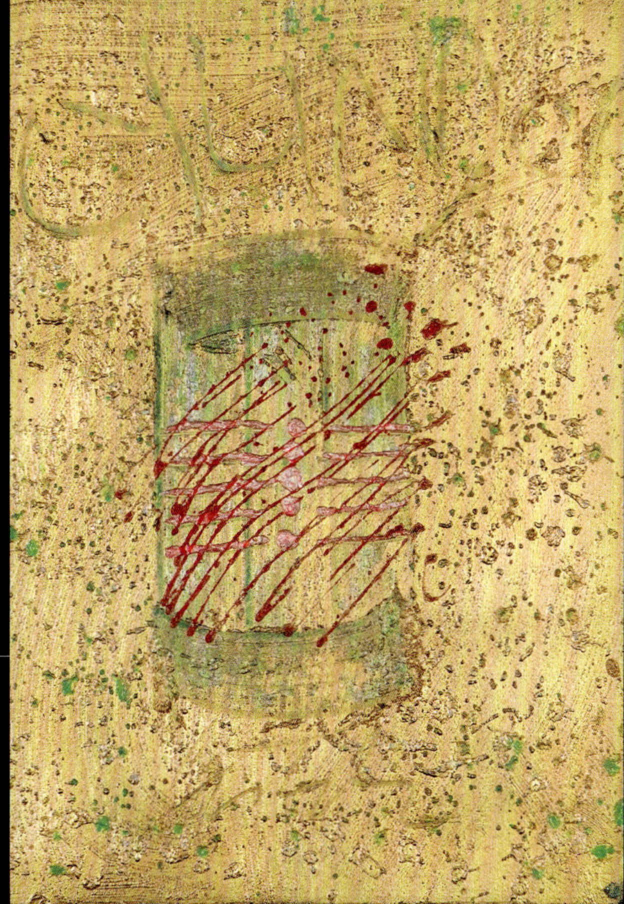

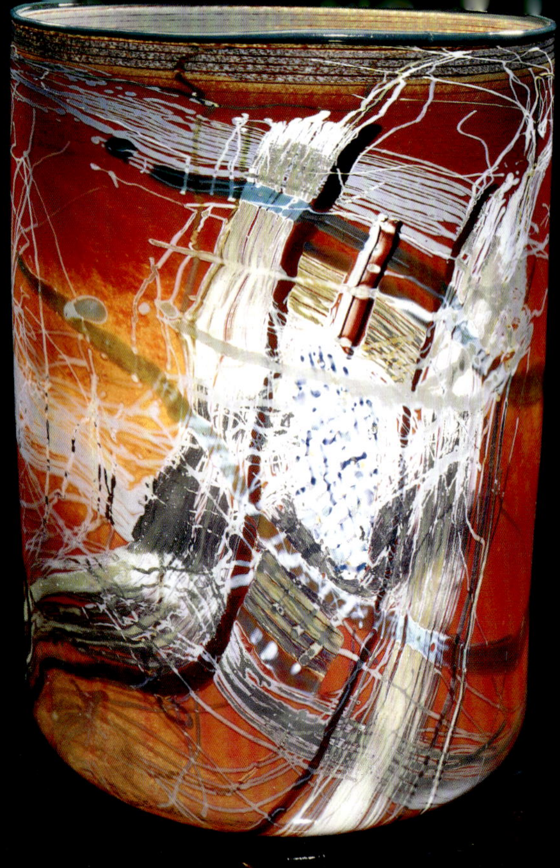

**Silver Gray Cylinder
with Deep Green Lip Wrap**

1984, 17 x 14 x 13"

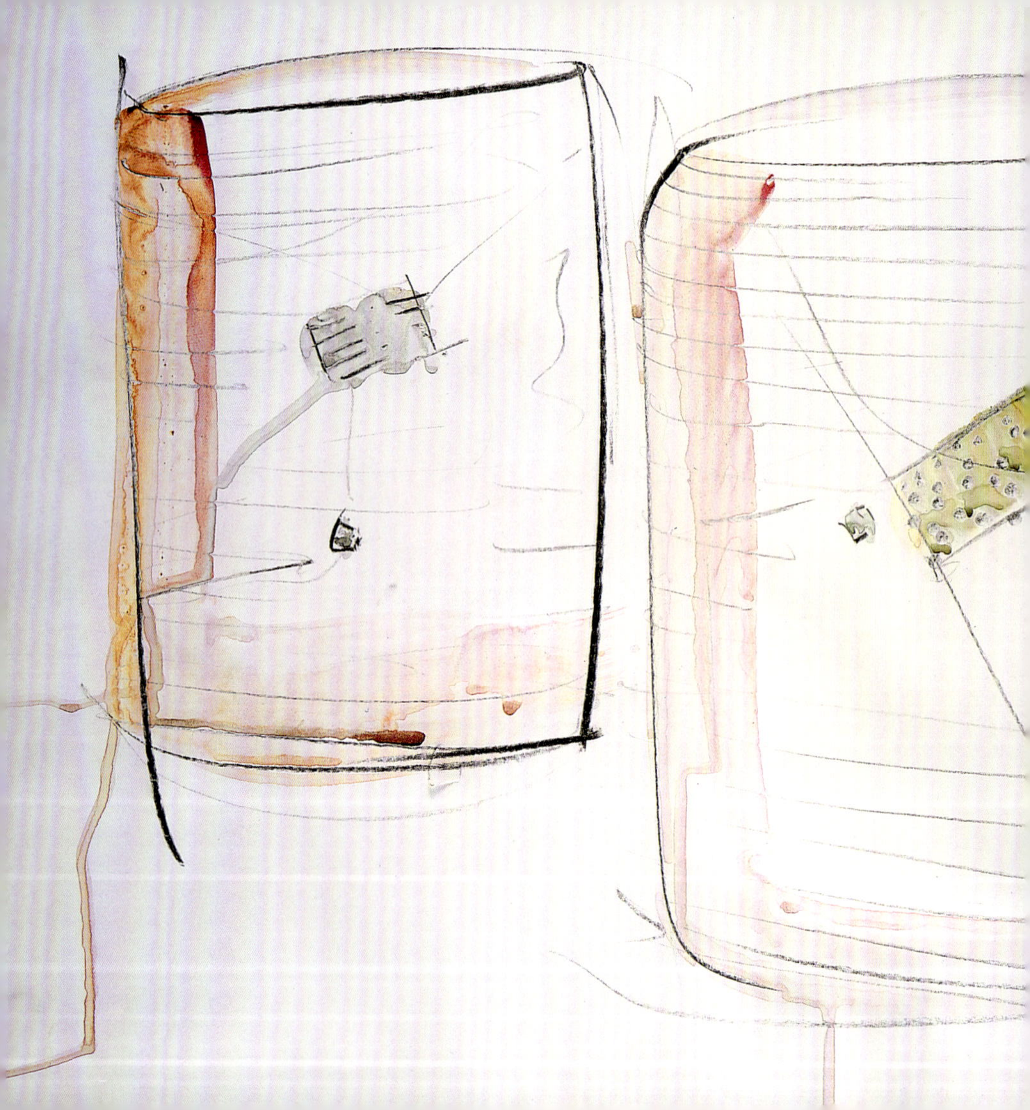

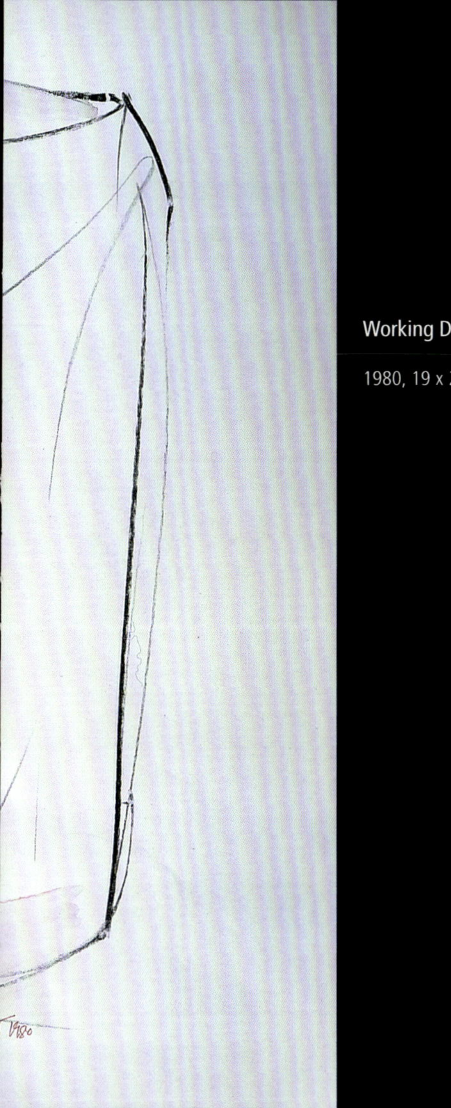

Working Drawing #272

1980, 19 x 26"

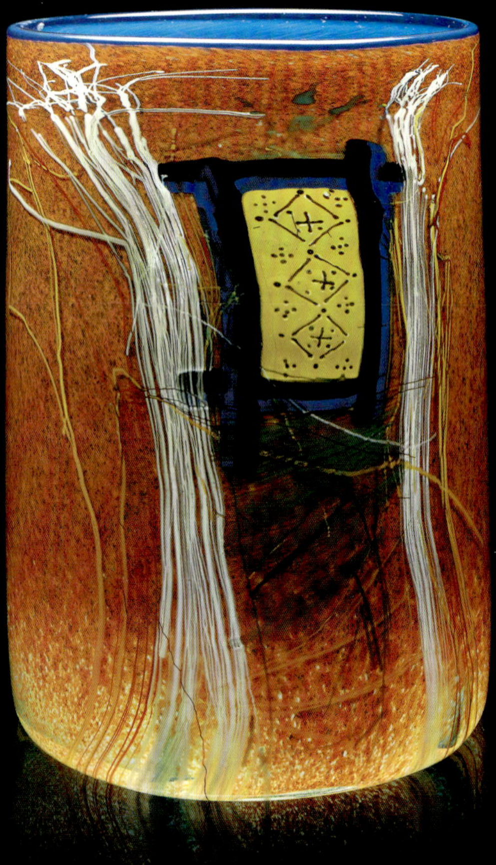

**Marine Blue
Cylinder with Royal
Blue Lip Wrap**

1984, 13 x 9"

**Sky Blue
Soft Cylinder
with Drawing**

1984, 10 x 12 x 12"

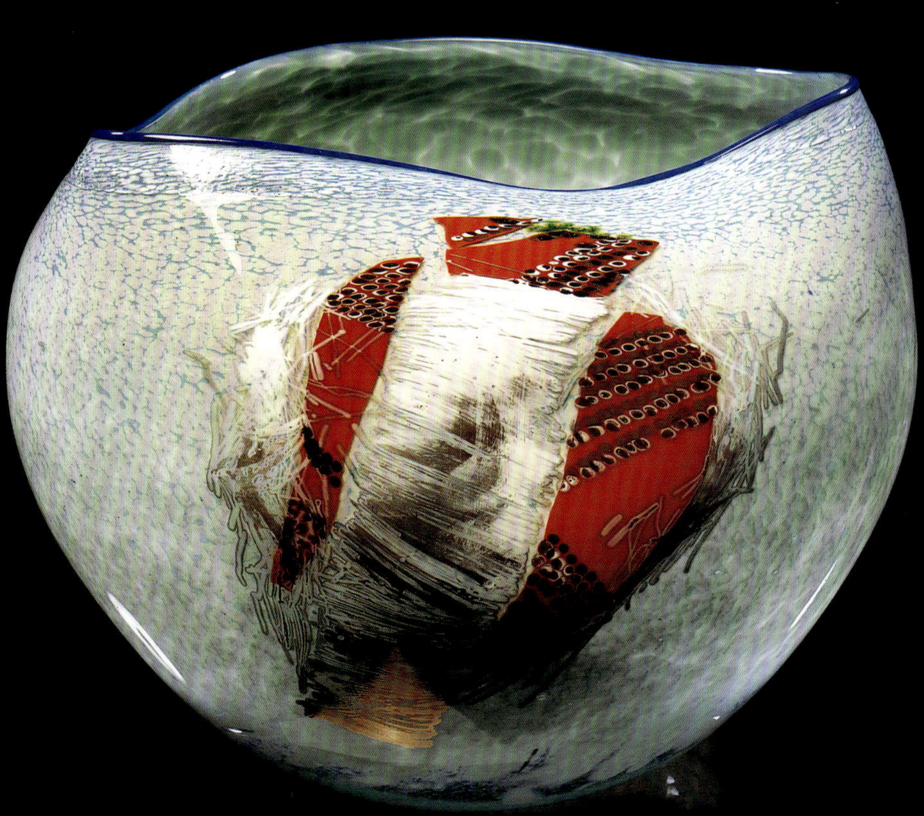

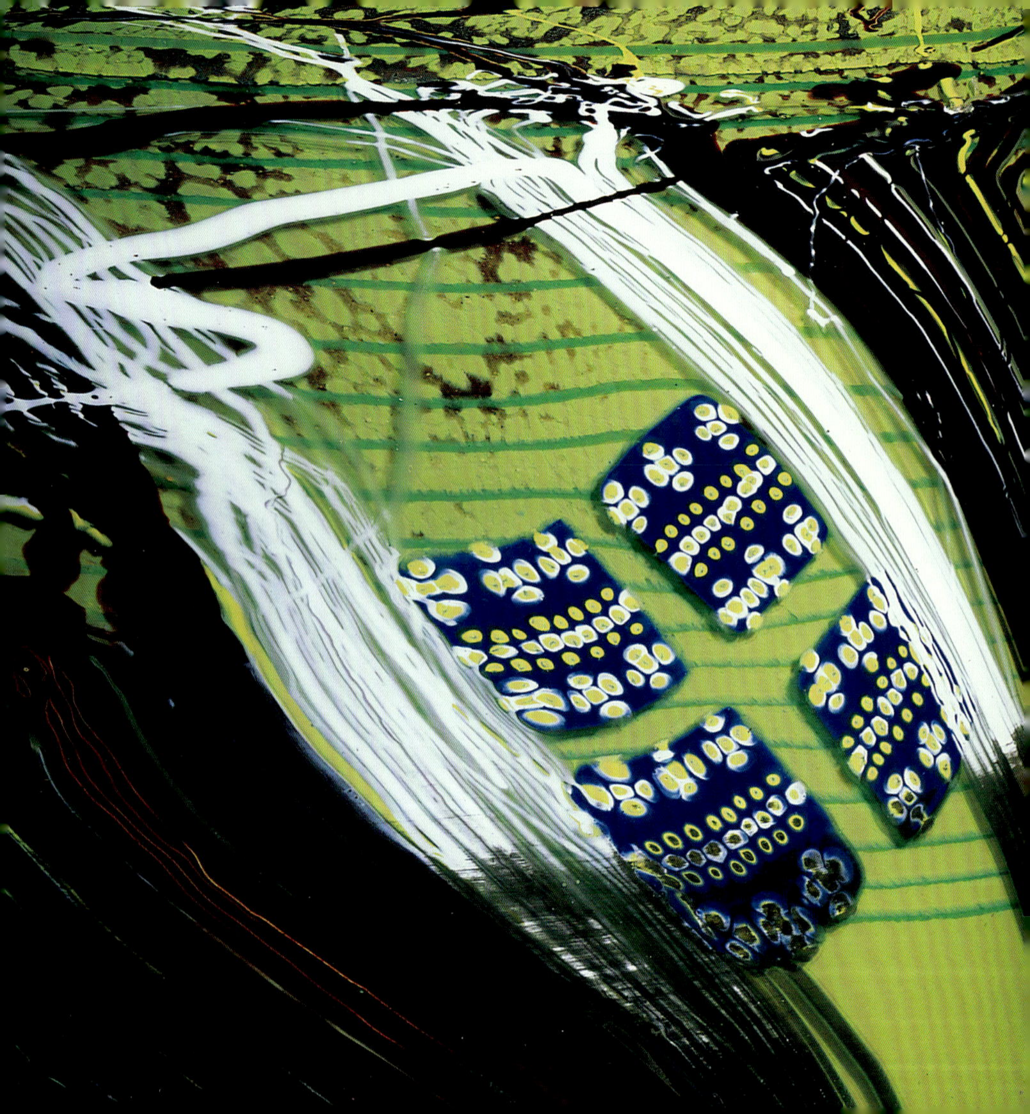

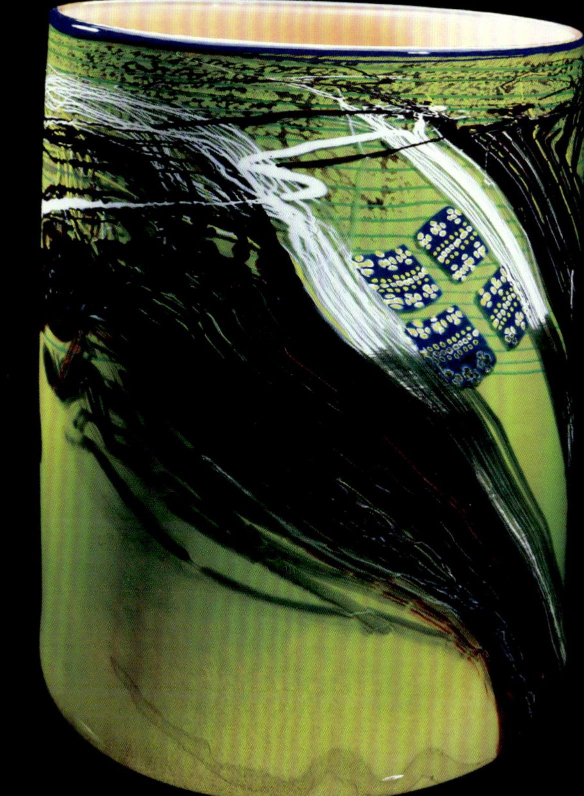

Spring Green Cylinder

1984, 14 x 11 x 11"

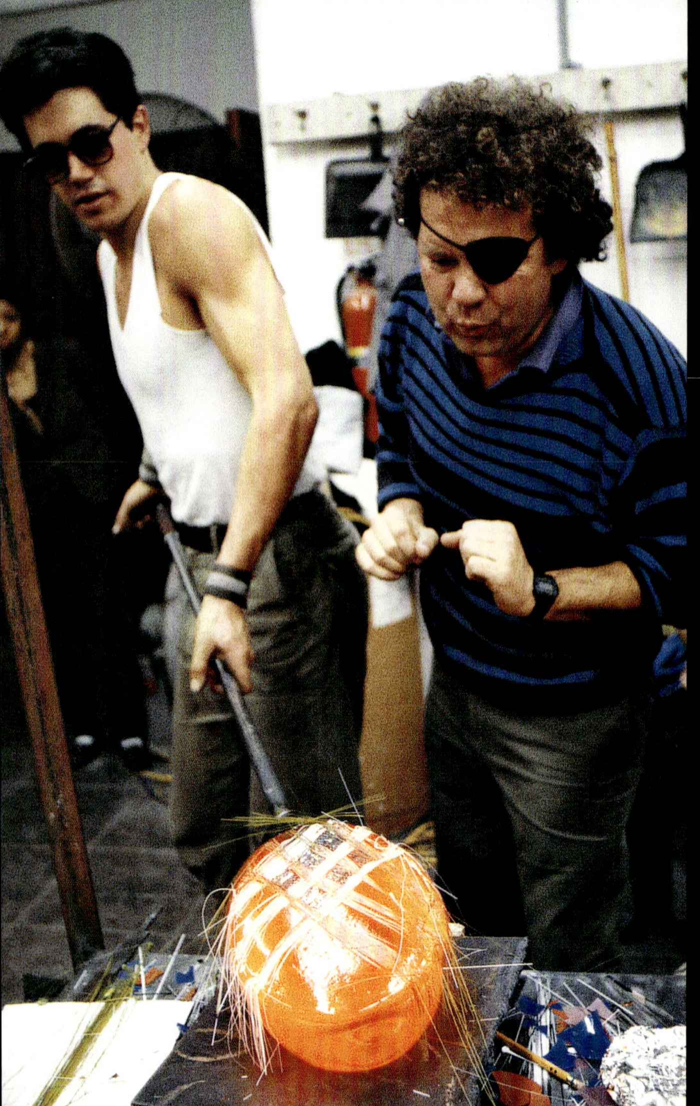

Rose Madder
Soft Cylinder with
Blue Lip Wrap

1984, 11 x 11 x 11"

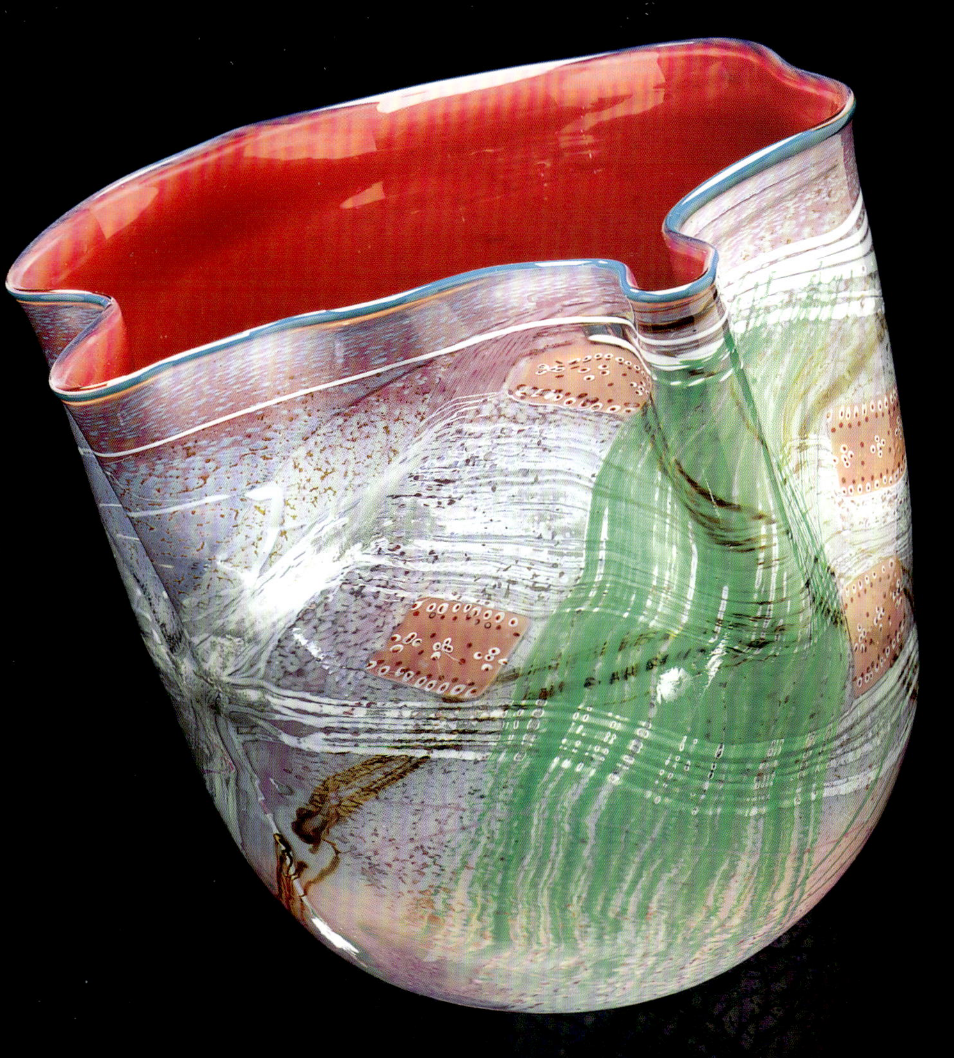

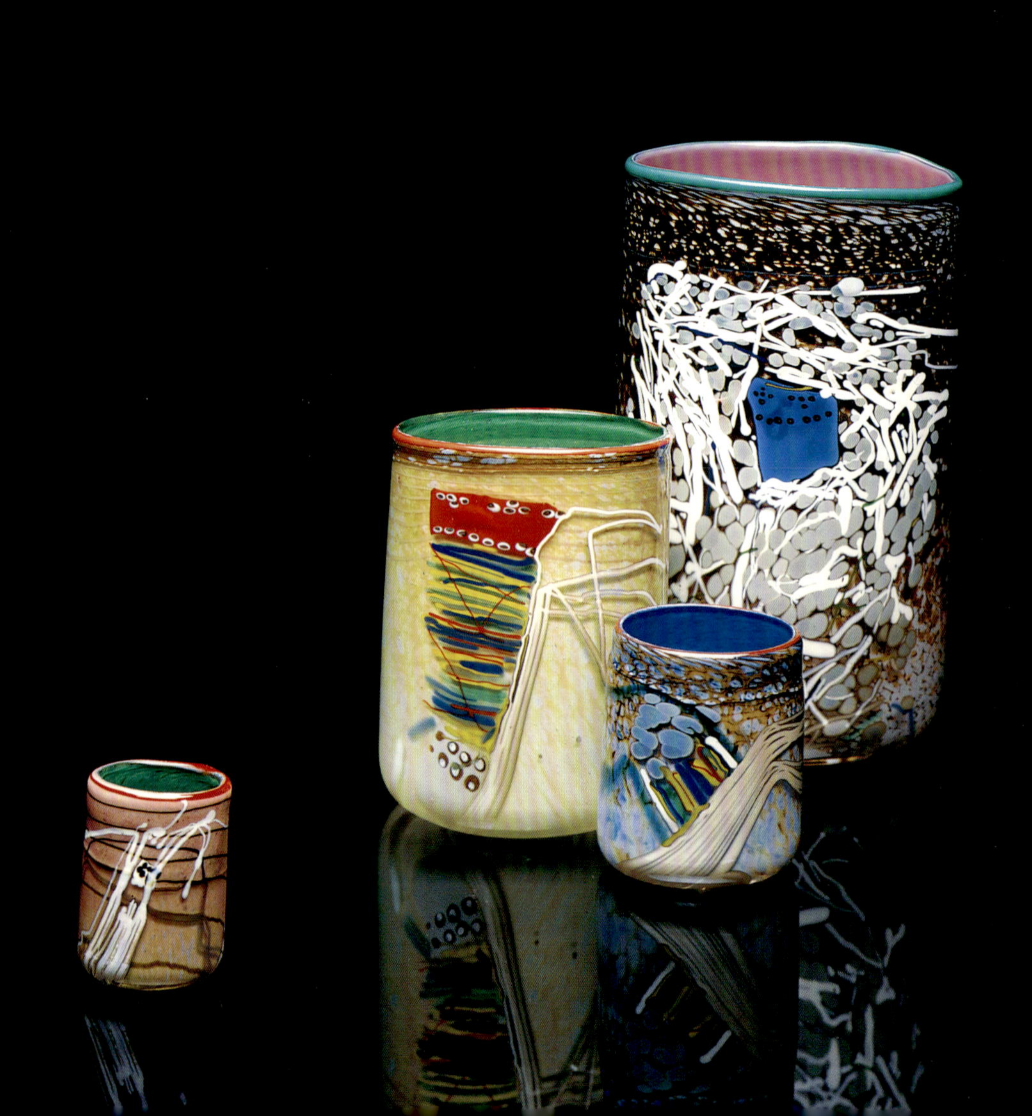

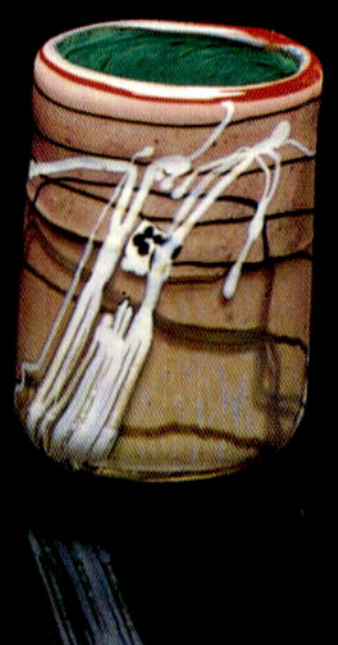

Cylinder Grouping

1984

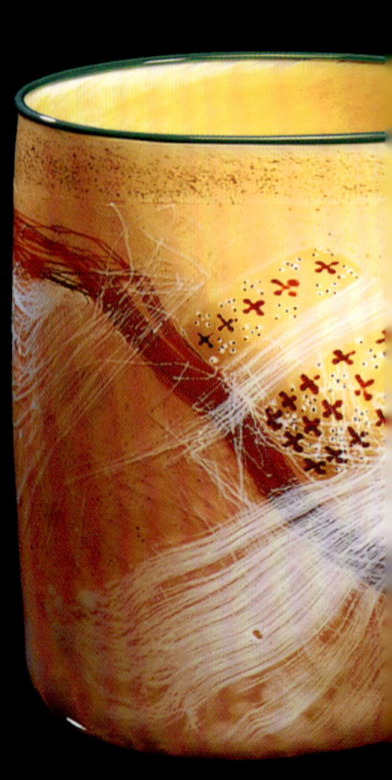

Cylinder Grouping

1984–87

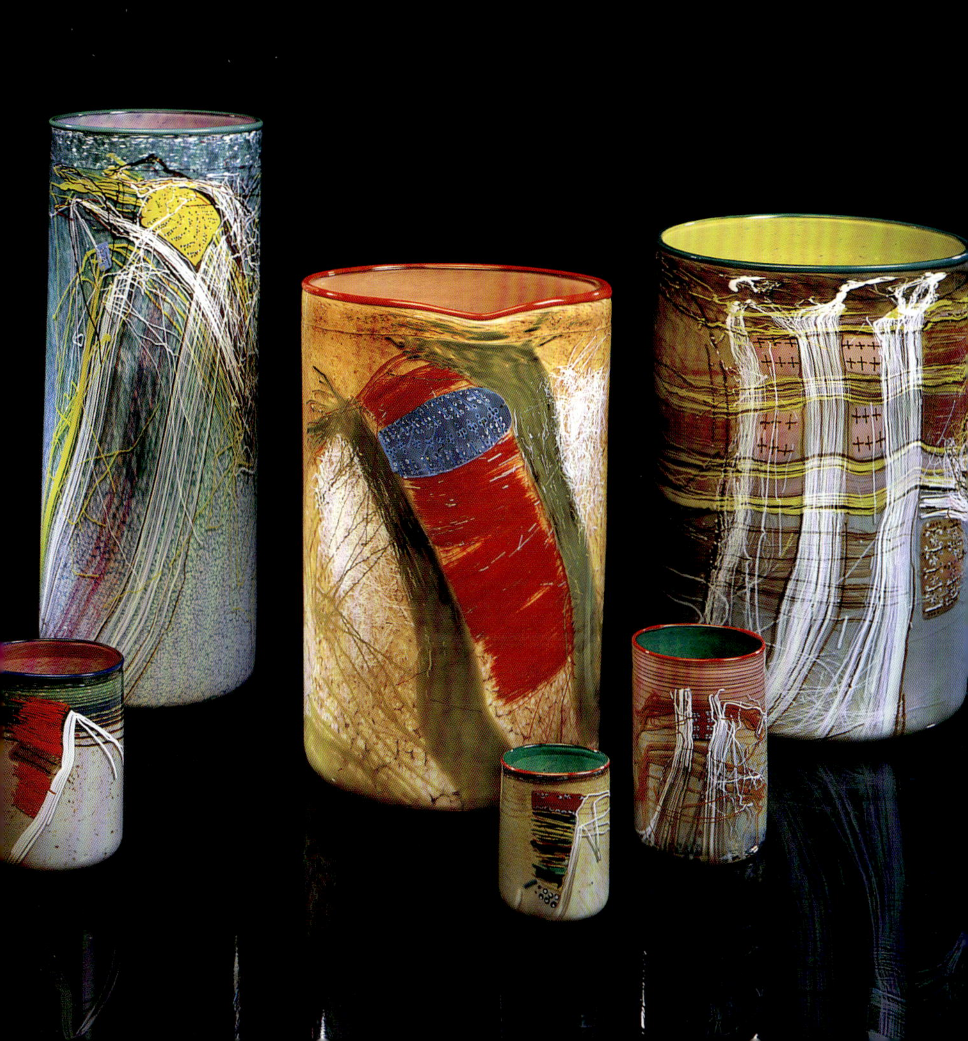

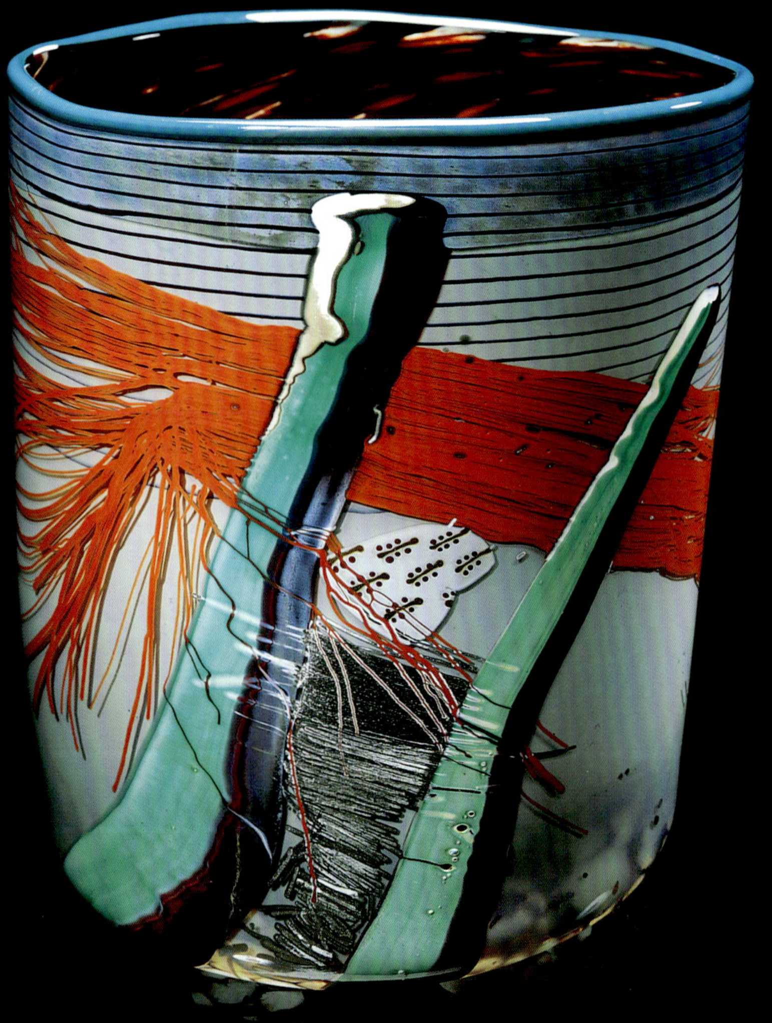

Pilchuck Cylinder

1984, 12 x 8"

Scarlet Cylinder
Drawing

2007, 30 x 22"

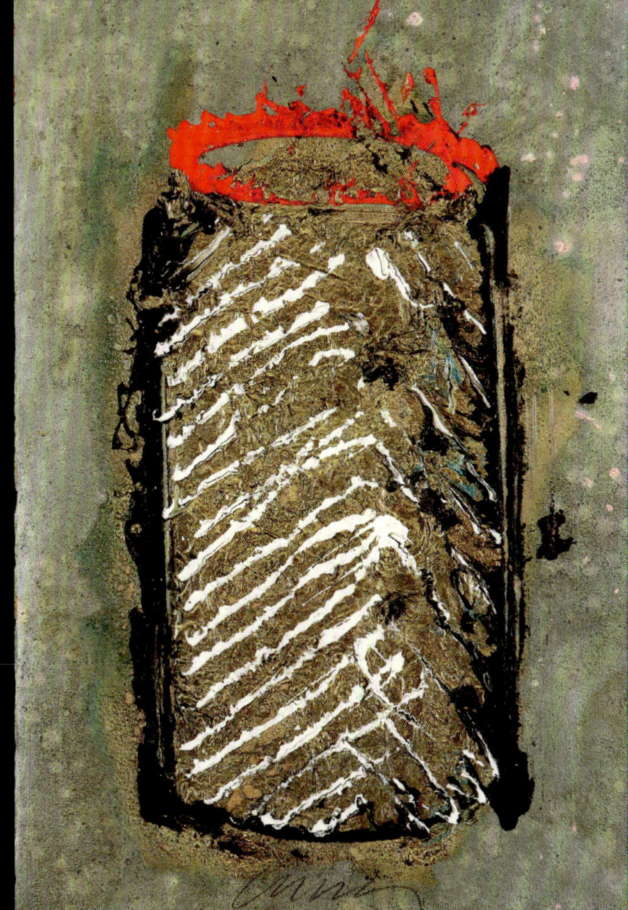

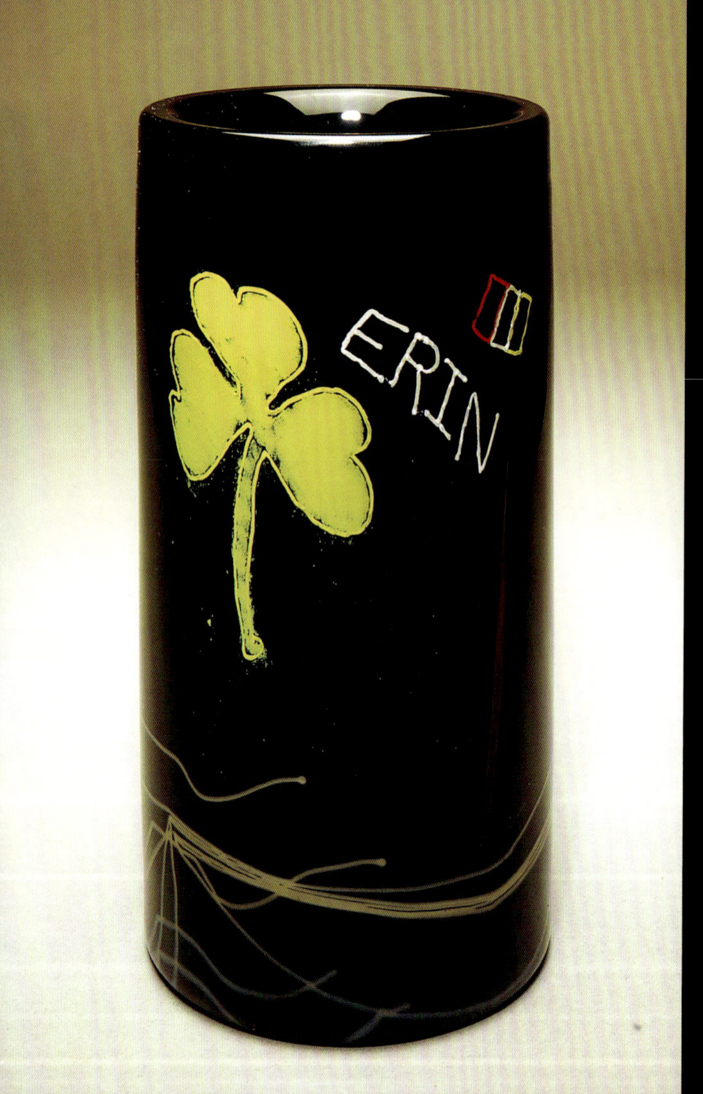

Black Irish
Cylinder #9

2006, 9 x 5 x 5"

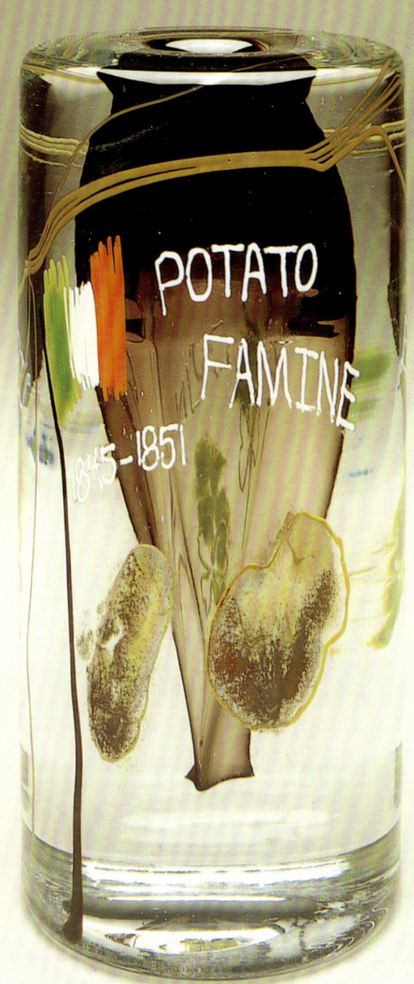

Black Irish
Cylinder #2

2006, 10 x 5 x 5"

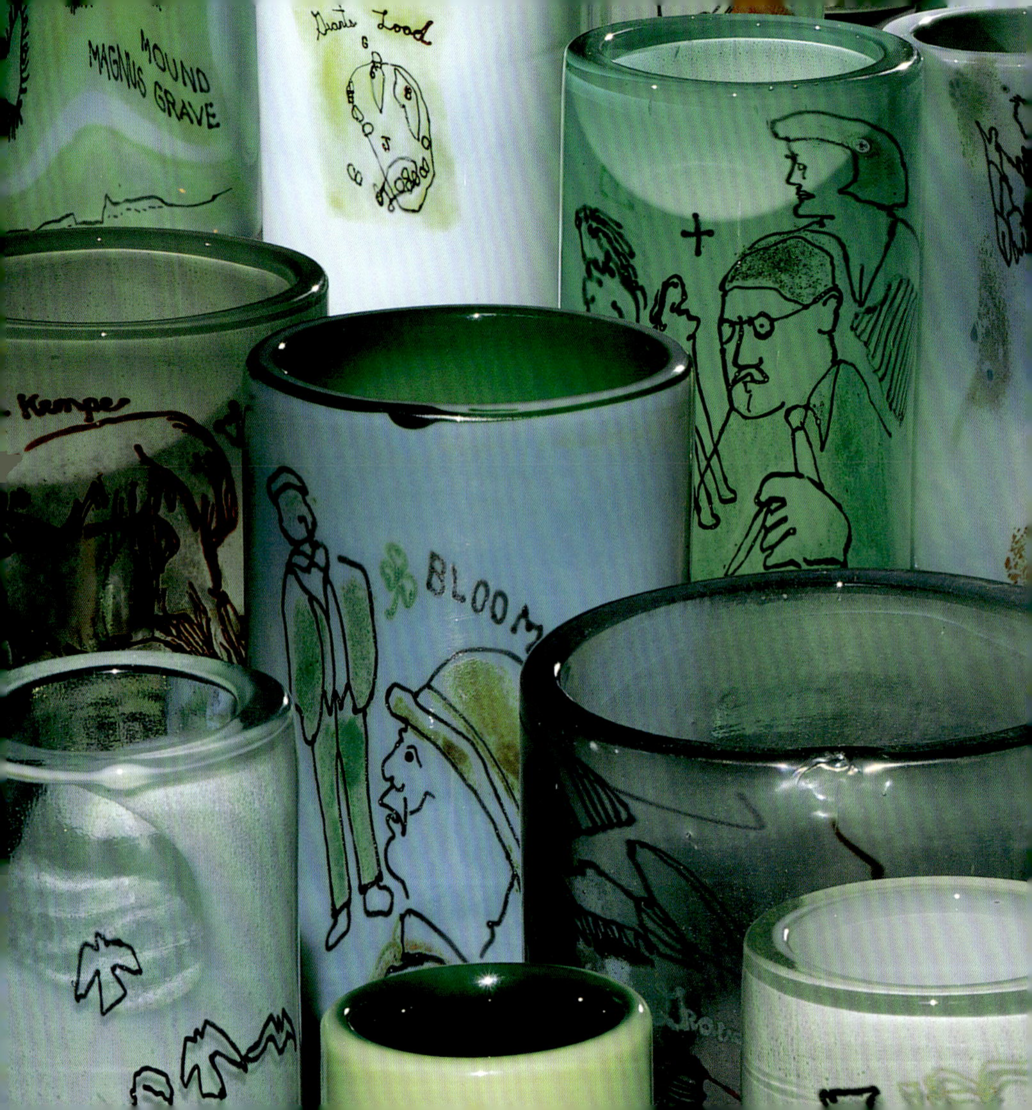
MOUND
MAGNUS GRAVE
Giant's Load
Kempe
BLOOM

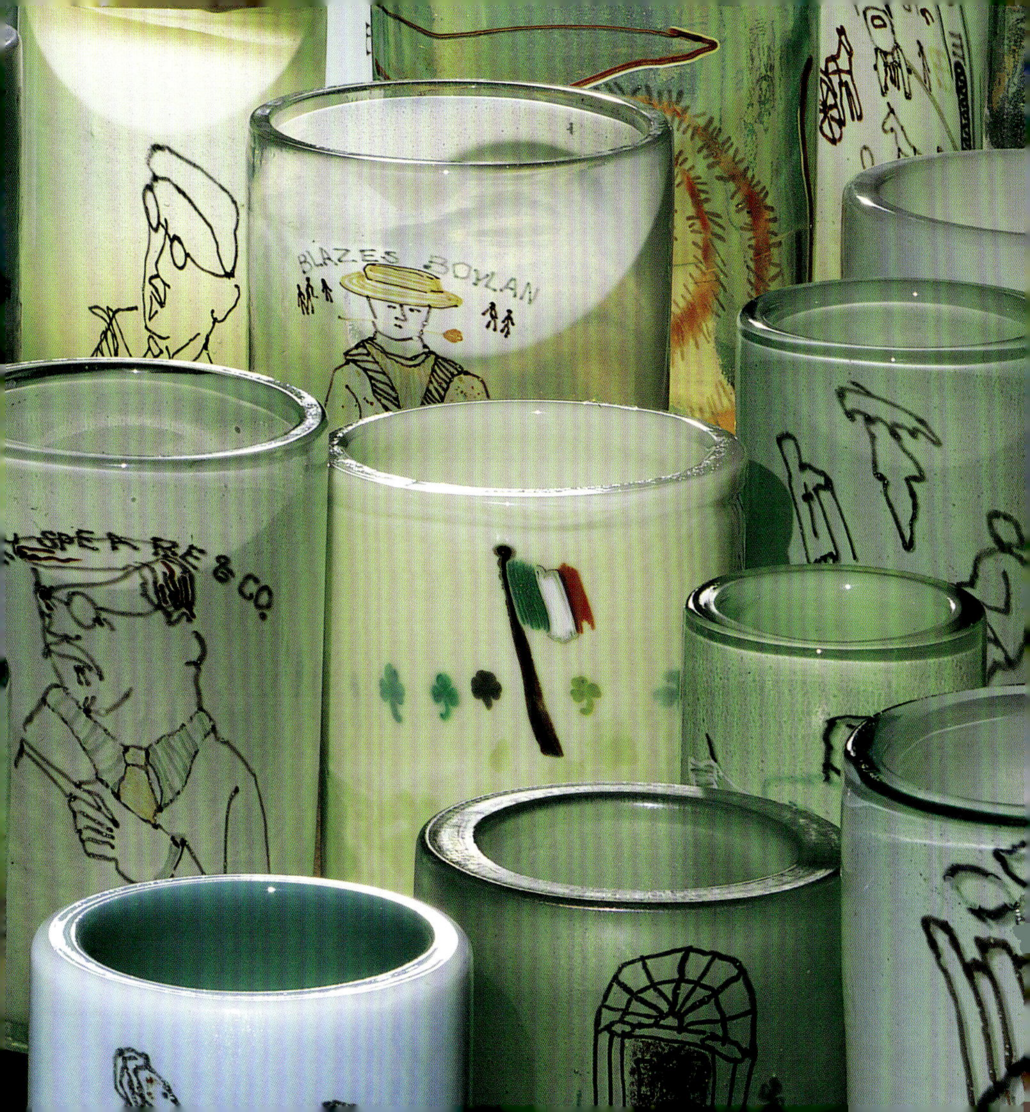
BLAZES BOYLAN
SPEARE & CO.

Preceding page:
Irish Cylinder Grouping

In collaboration with Seaver Leslie
1975

Flora C. Mace

Rhode Island School of Design
Providence, Rhode Island, 1976

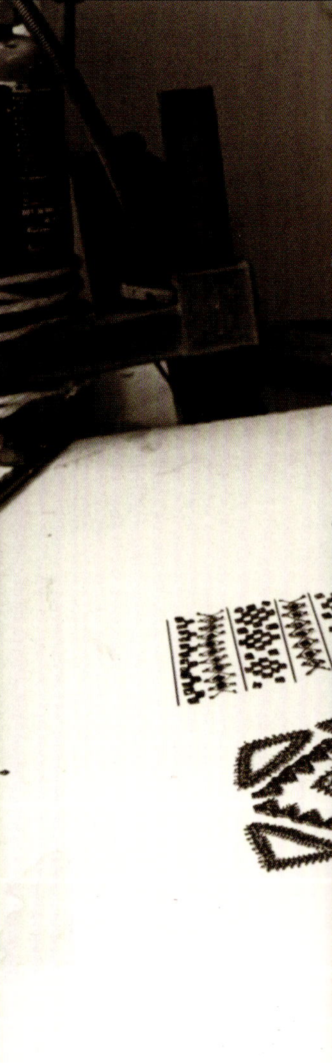

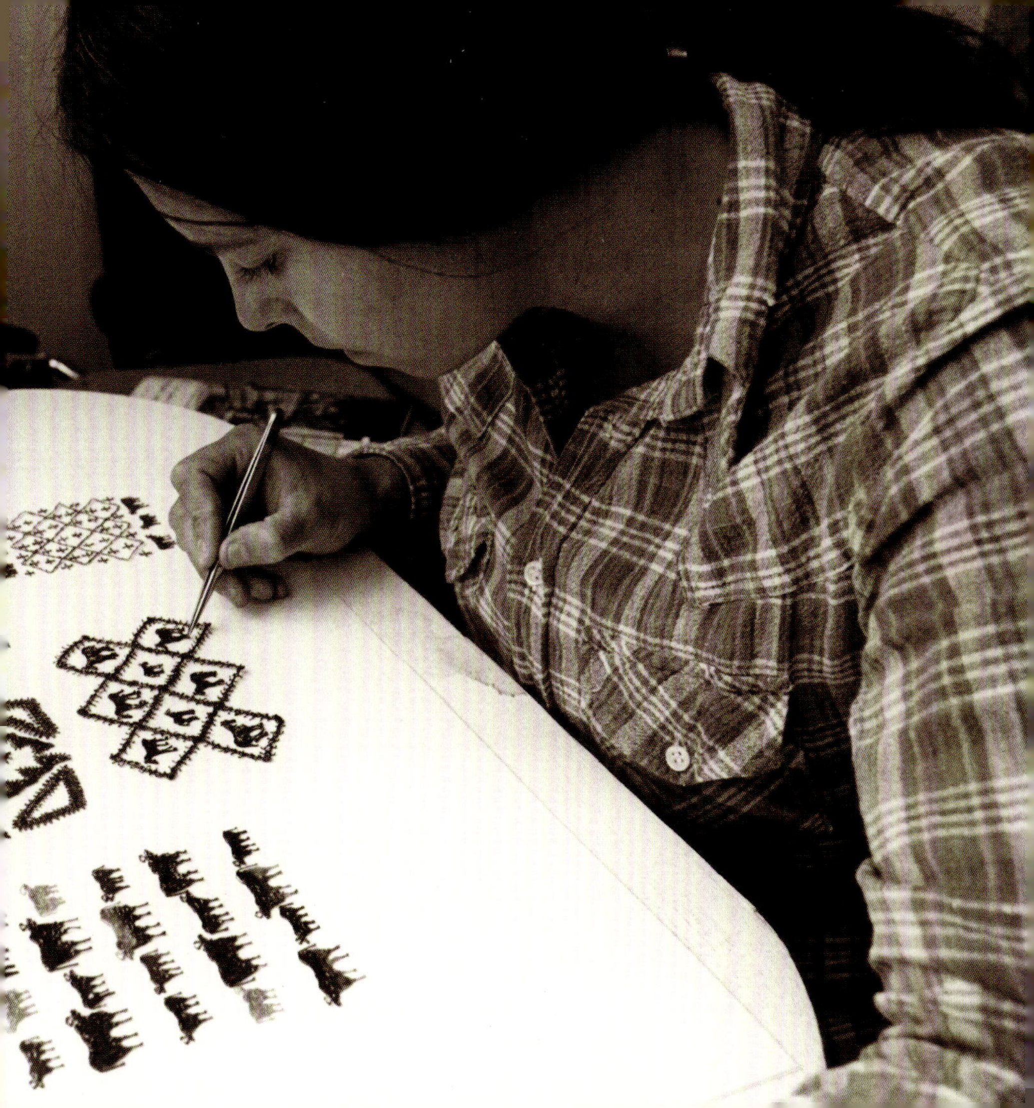

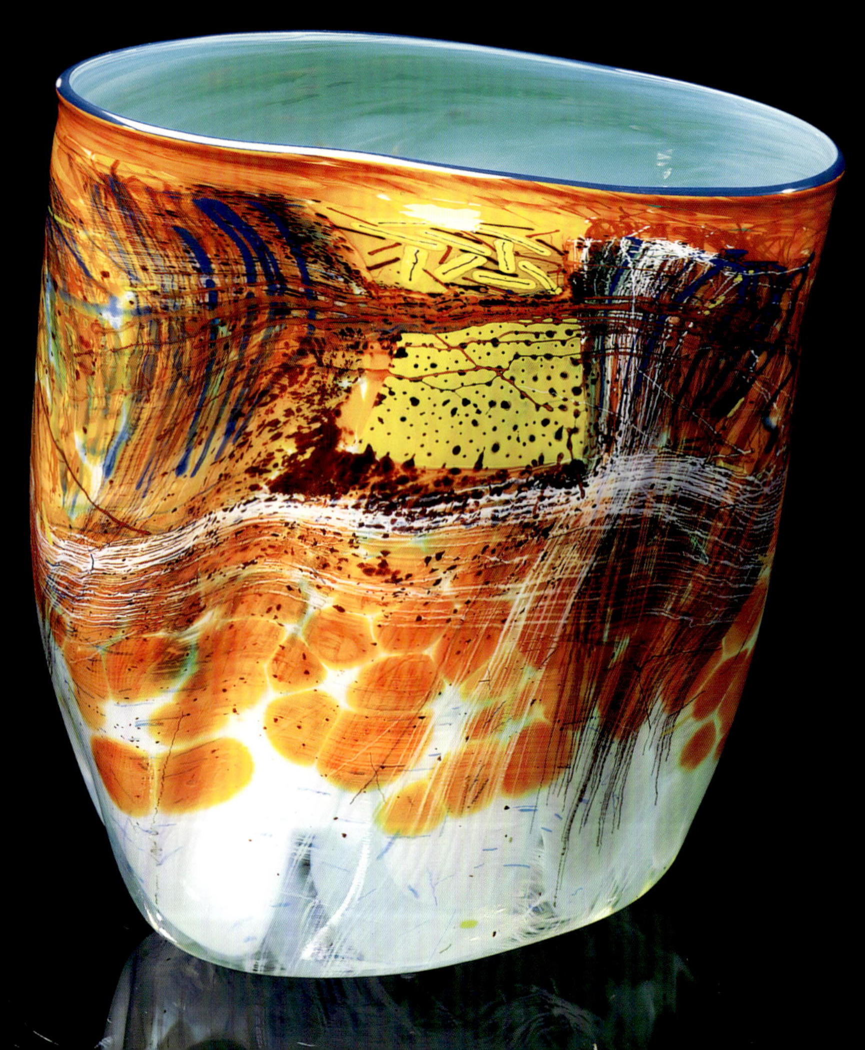

Turquoise Green Soft Cylinder
with Ochre Drawing

1988, 17 x 17 x 14"

Following page:
Delta Yellow Soft Cylinder
with Red Ochre Drawing

1986, 14 x 12 x 10"

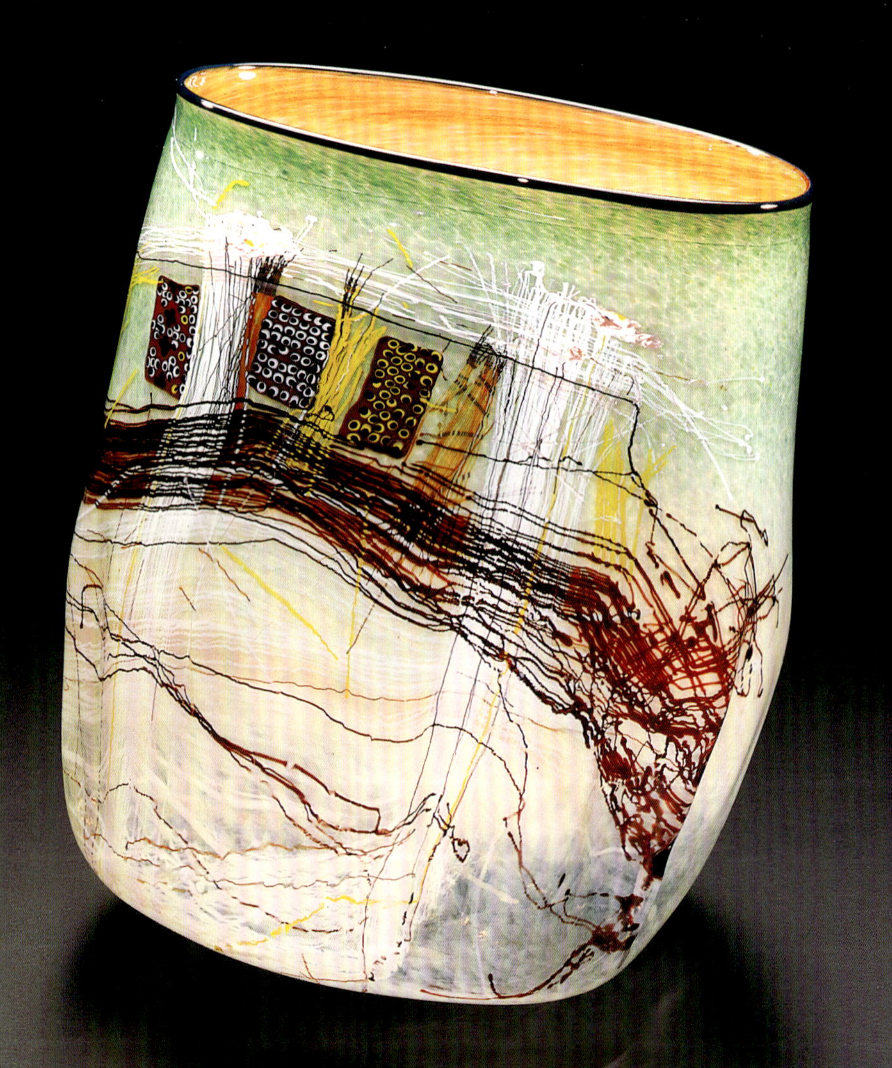

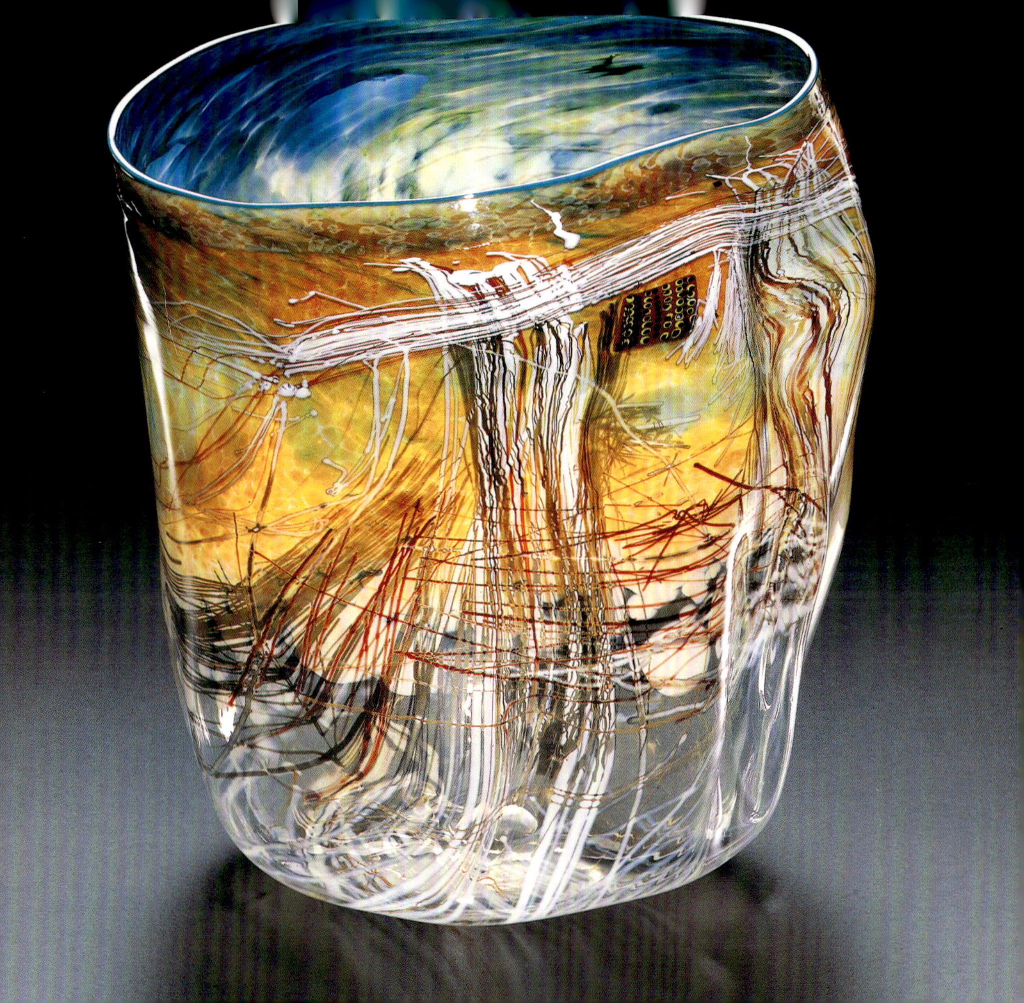

Cylinder Drawing

1977, 11 x 15"

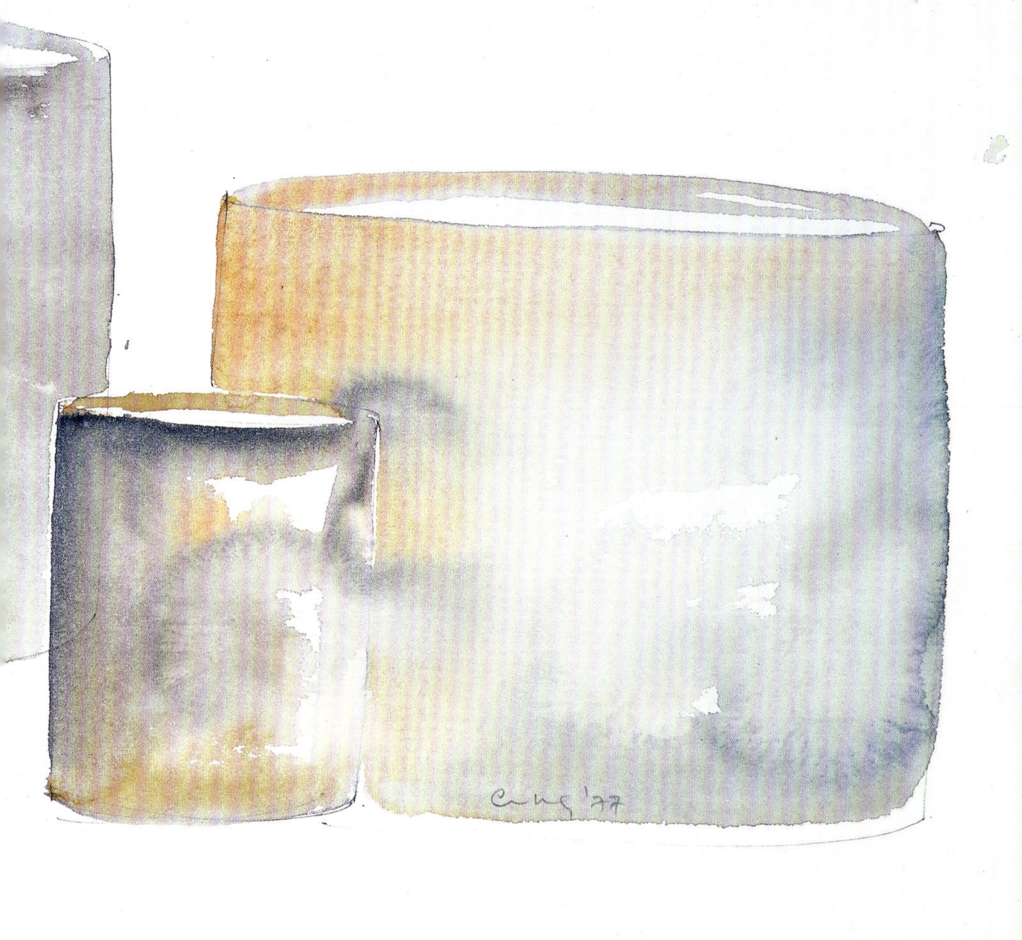

crg '77

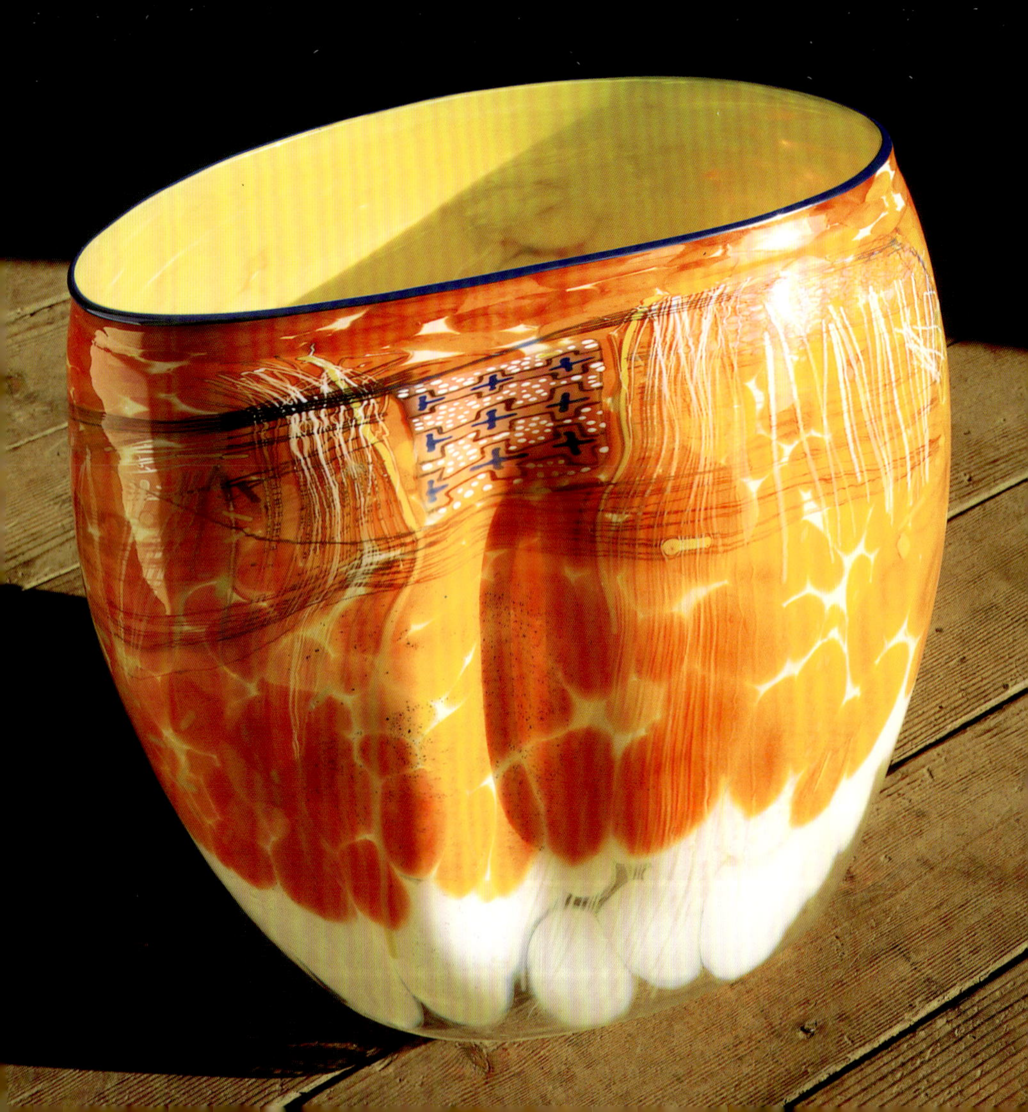

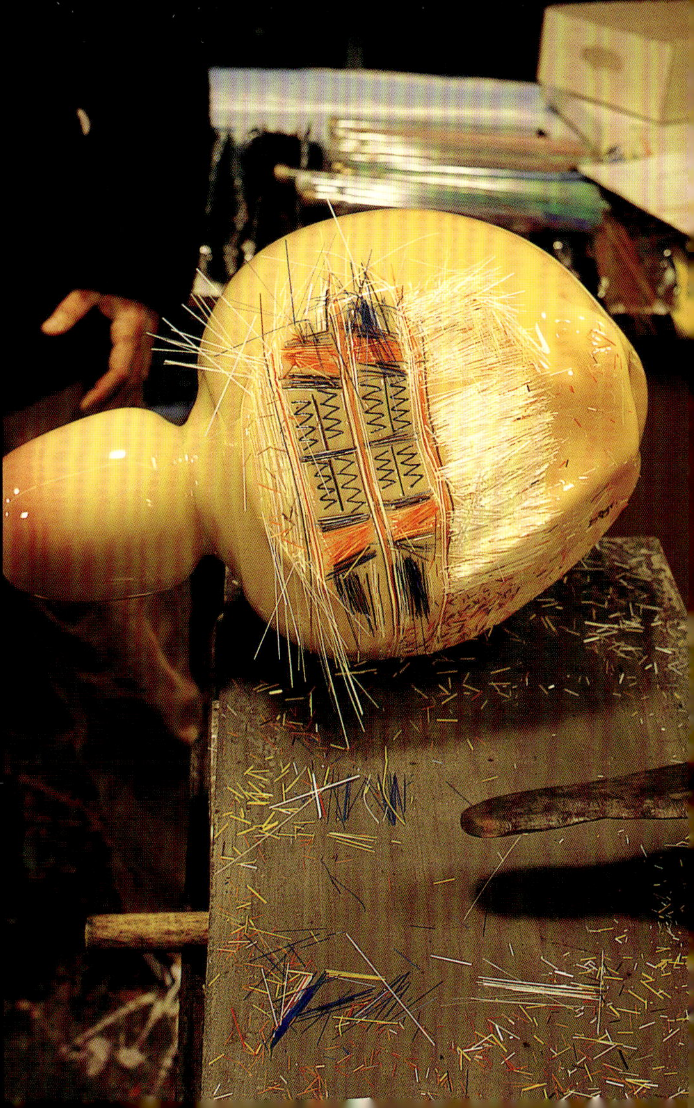

Soft Yellow Soft
Cylinder with Navy
Blue Lip Wrap

1988, 17 x 16 x 13"

"Picking up"
a drawing made
of glass threads

The Boathouse hotshop
Seattle, Washington, 1995

Peach Cylinders

1995

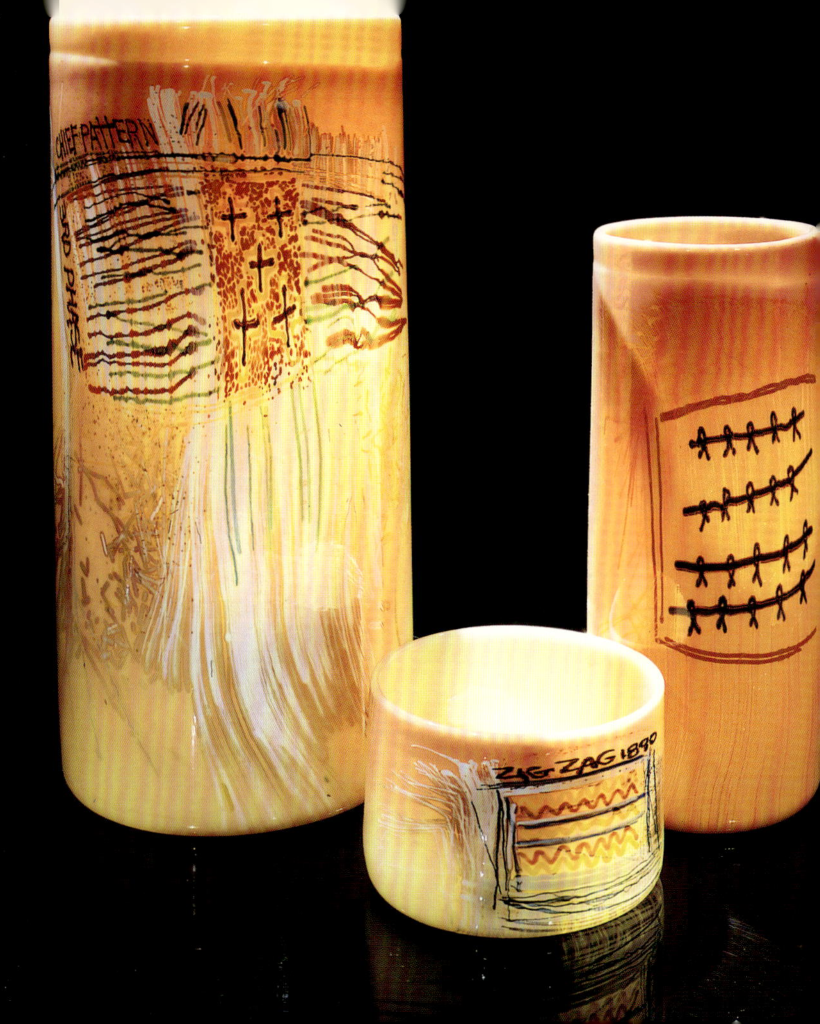
CHIEF PATTERN
3RD PHASE
ZIG ZAG 1890

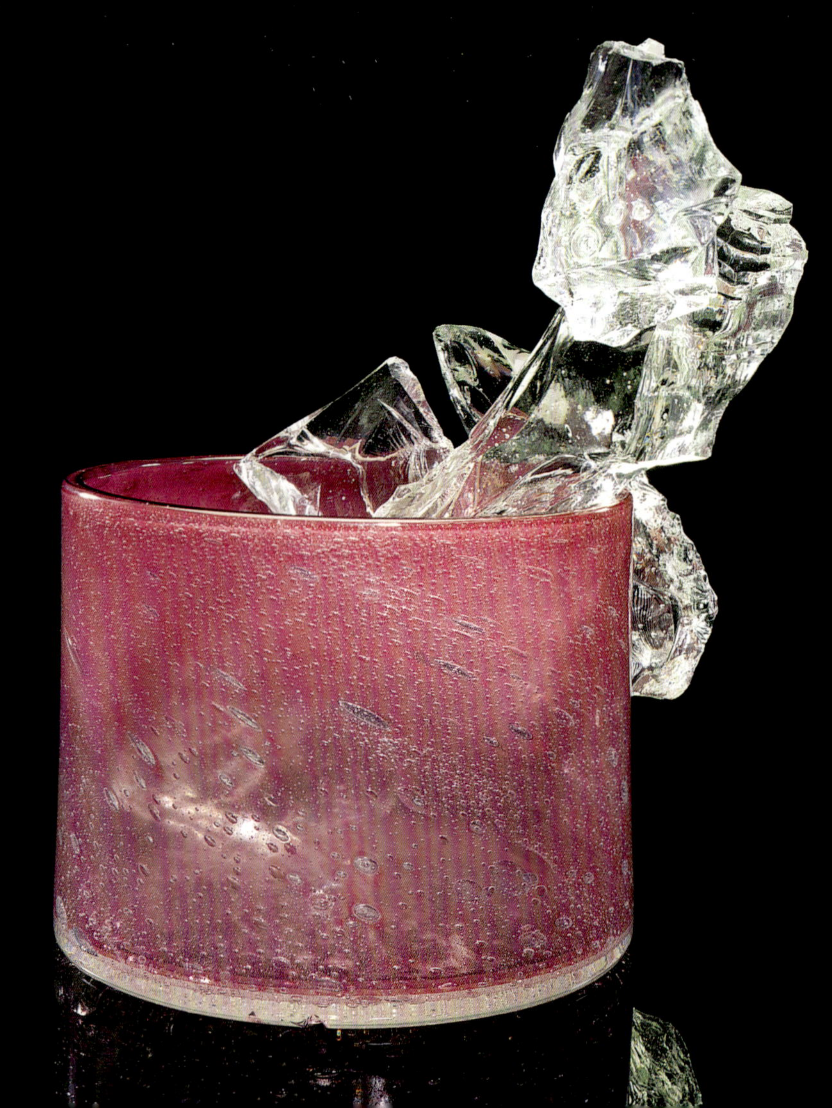

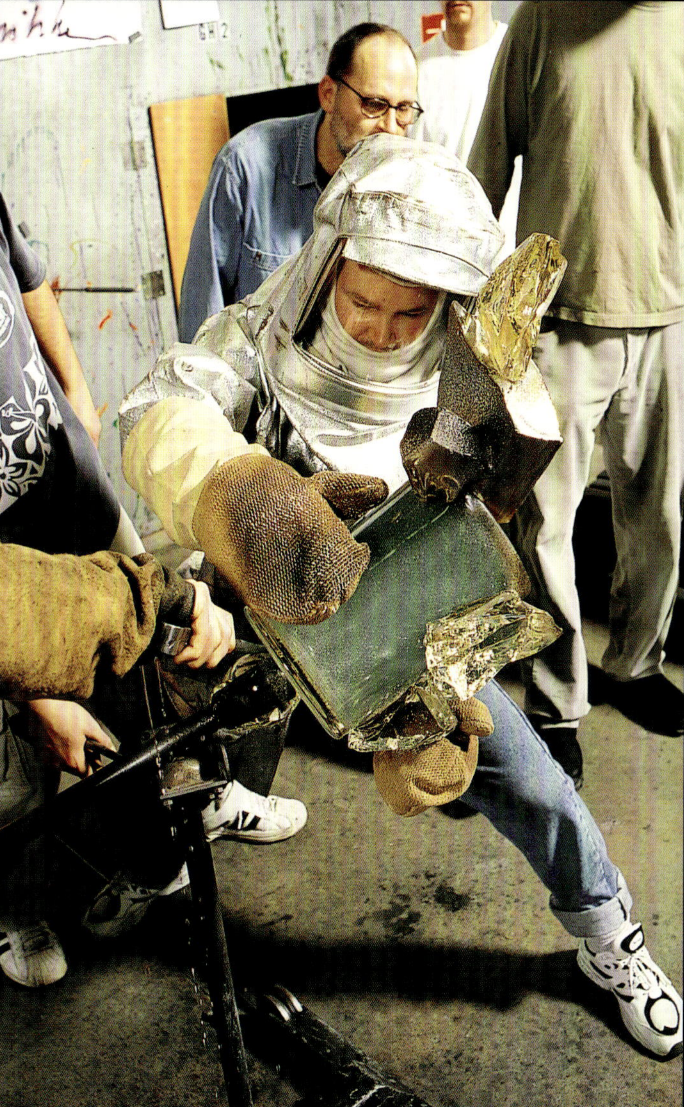

Jerusalem 2000
Cylinder #122

1999, 19 x 18 x 17"

Charles Parriott
and Jason Mouer

The Boathouse hotshop
Seattle, Washington, 1999

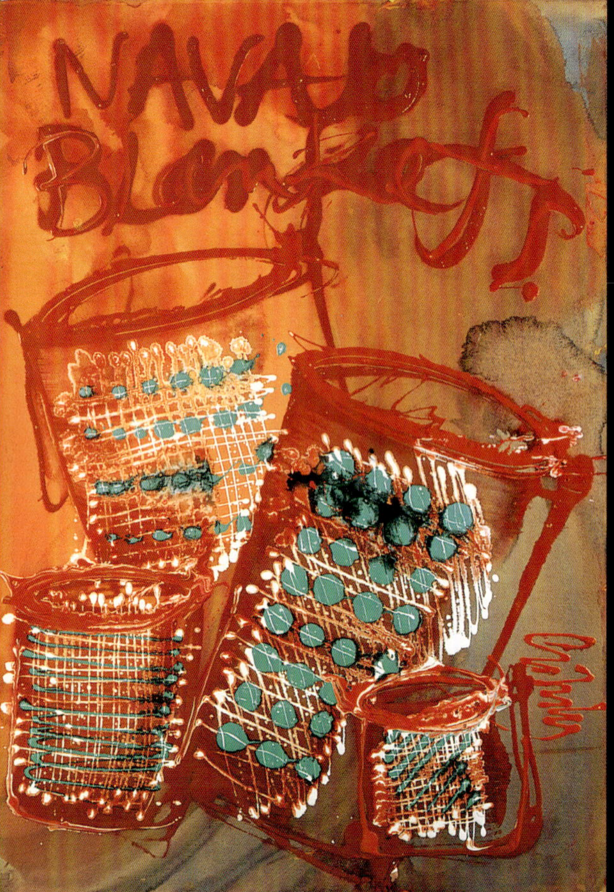

Navajo Blanket
Cylinder Drawing

1995, 42 x 30"

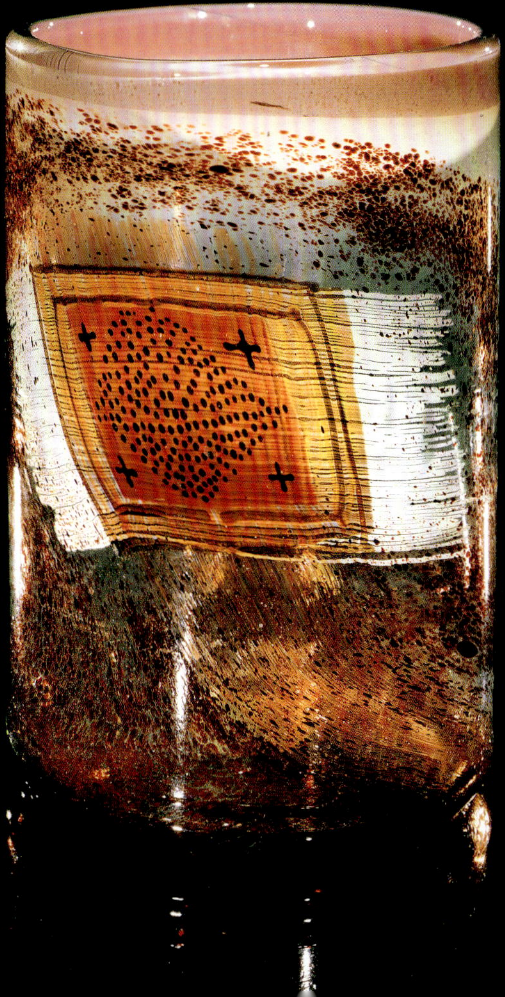

**Navajo Blanket
Cylinder**

1984, 11 x 8 x 8"

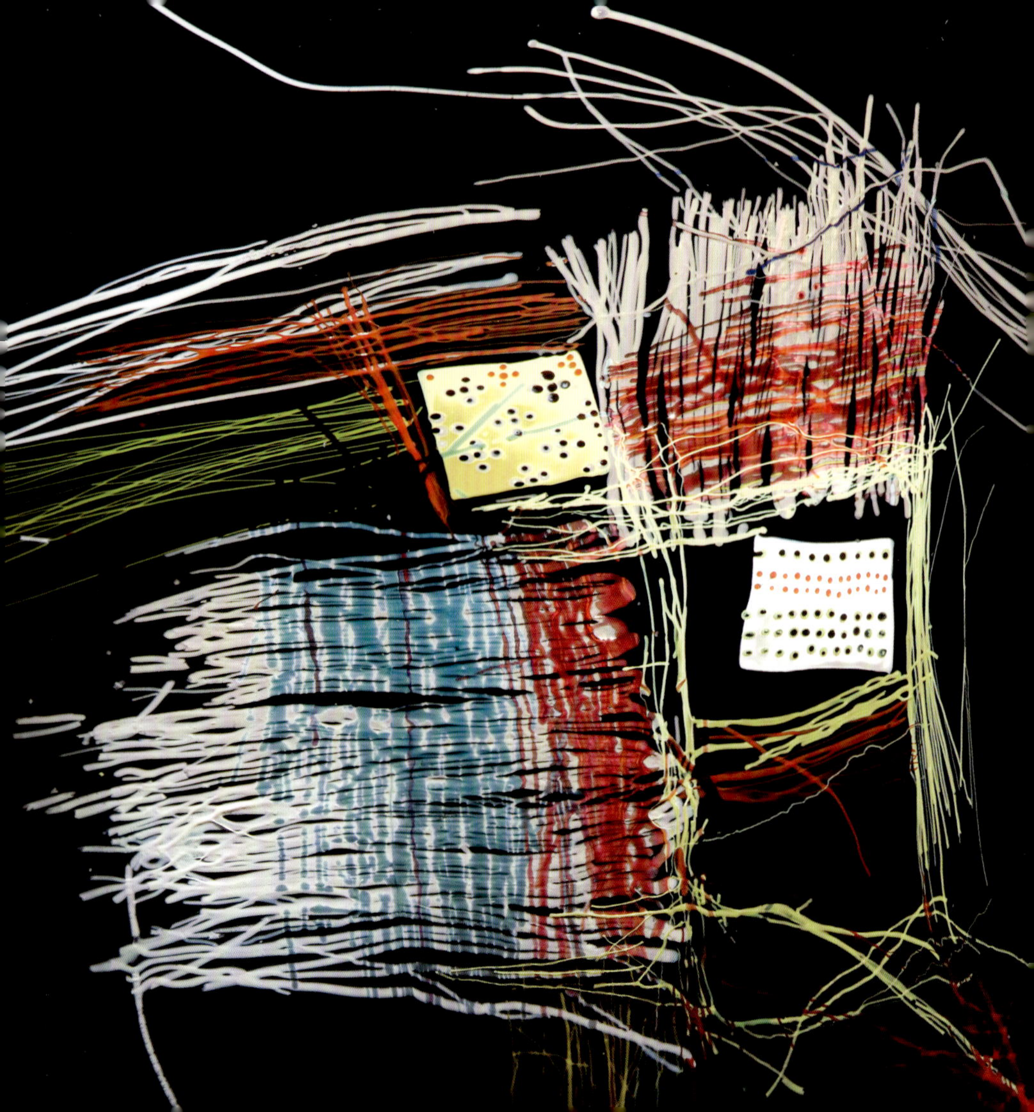

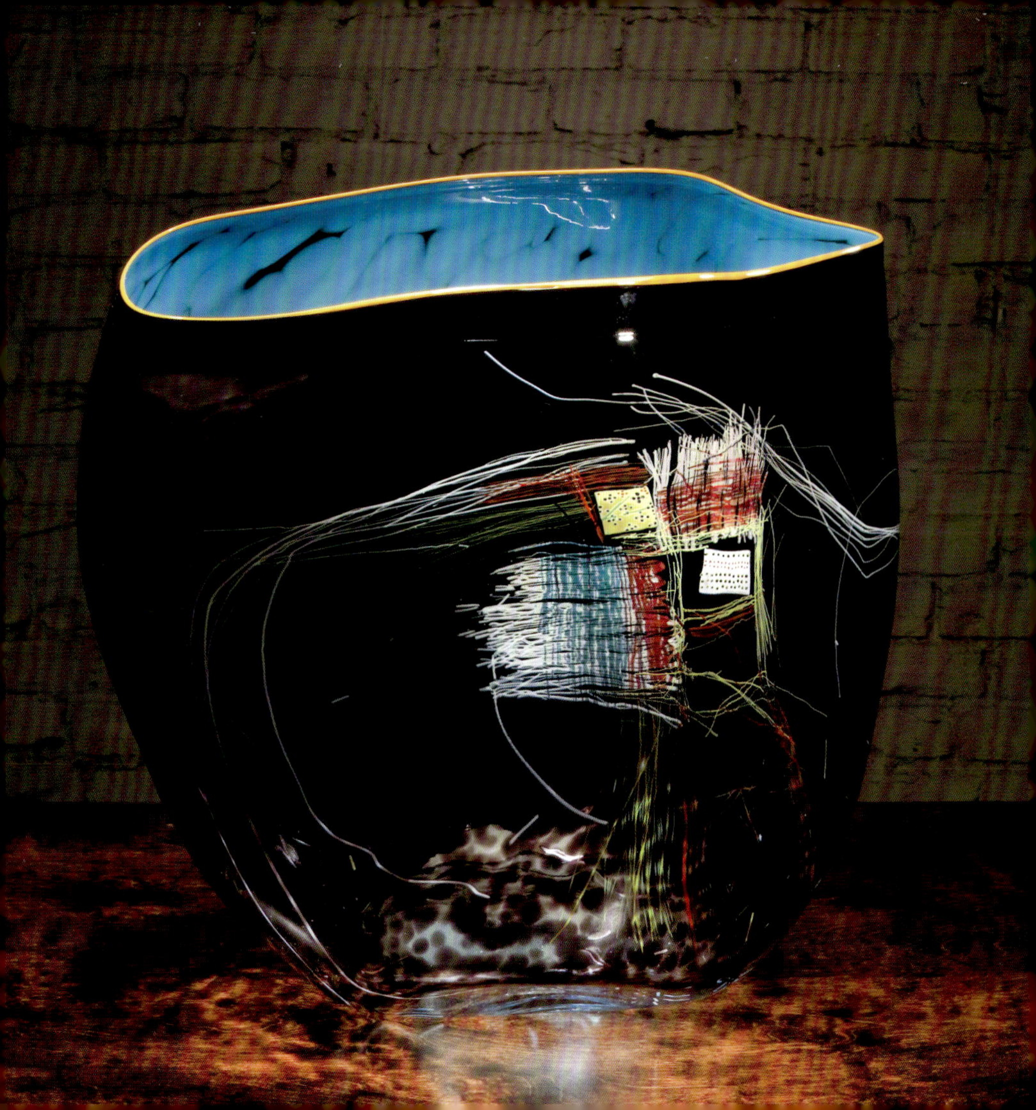

Preceding pages:
Black and Sky Blue Soft Cylinder
with Bright Yellow Lip Wrap

2008, 24 x 22 x 21"

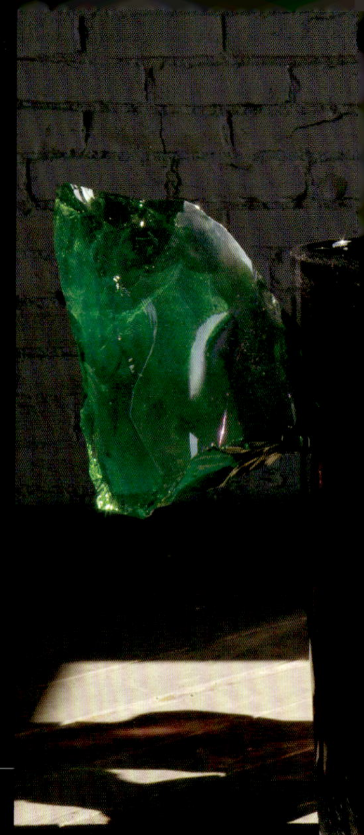

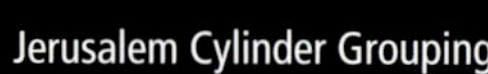

Jerusalem Cylinder Grouping

2007

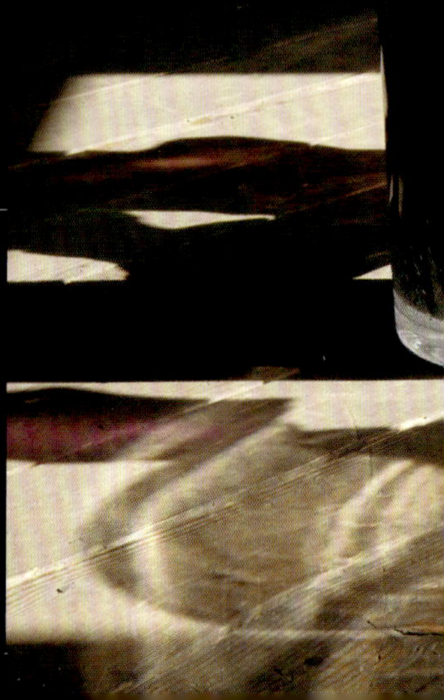

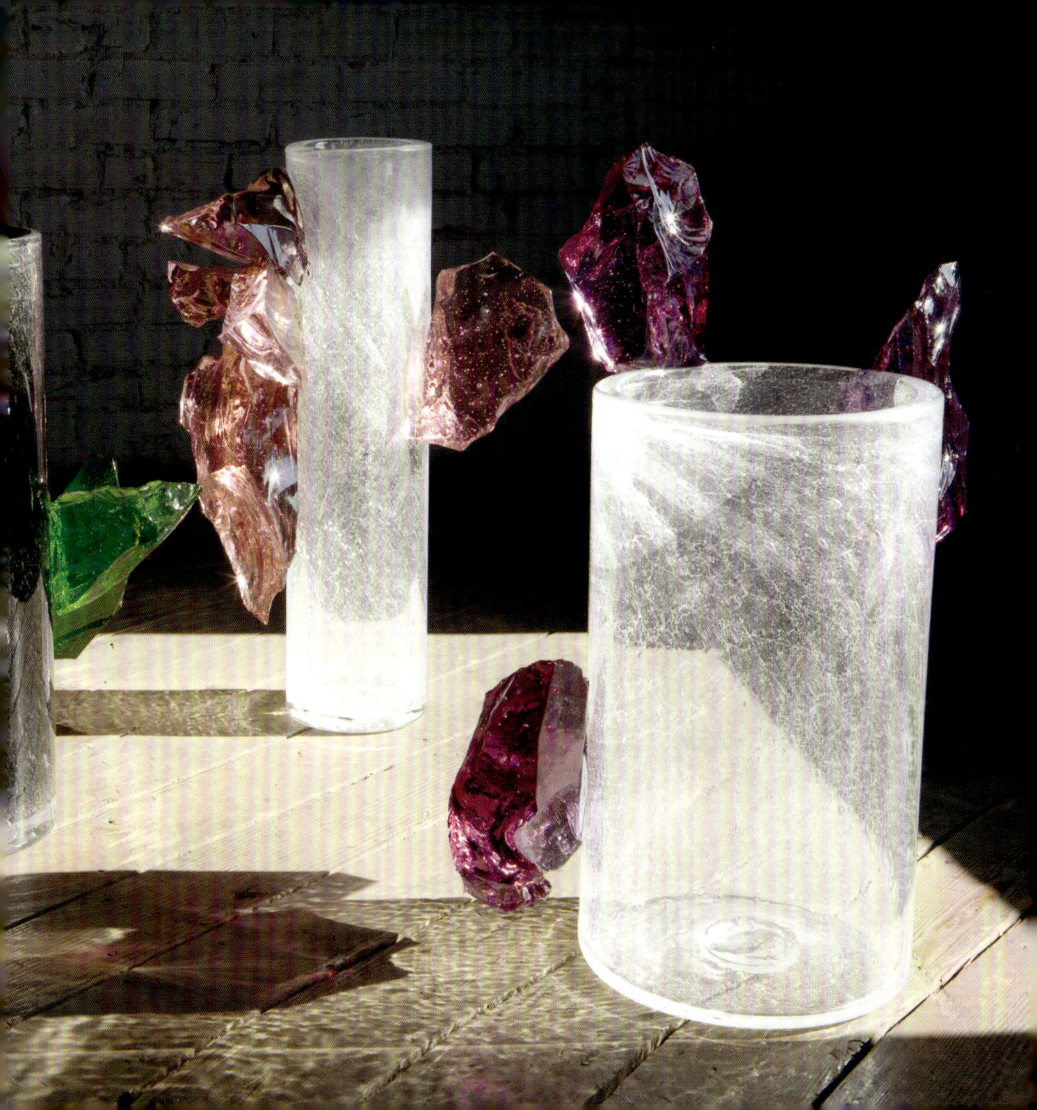

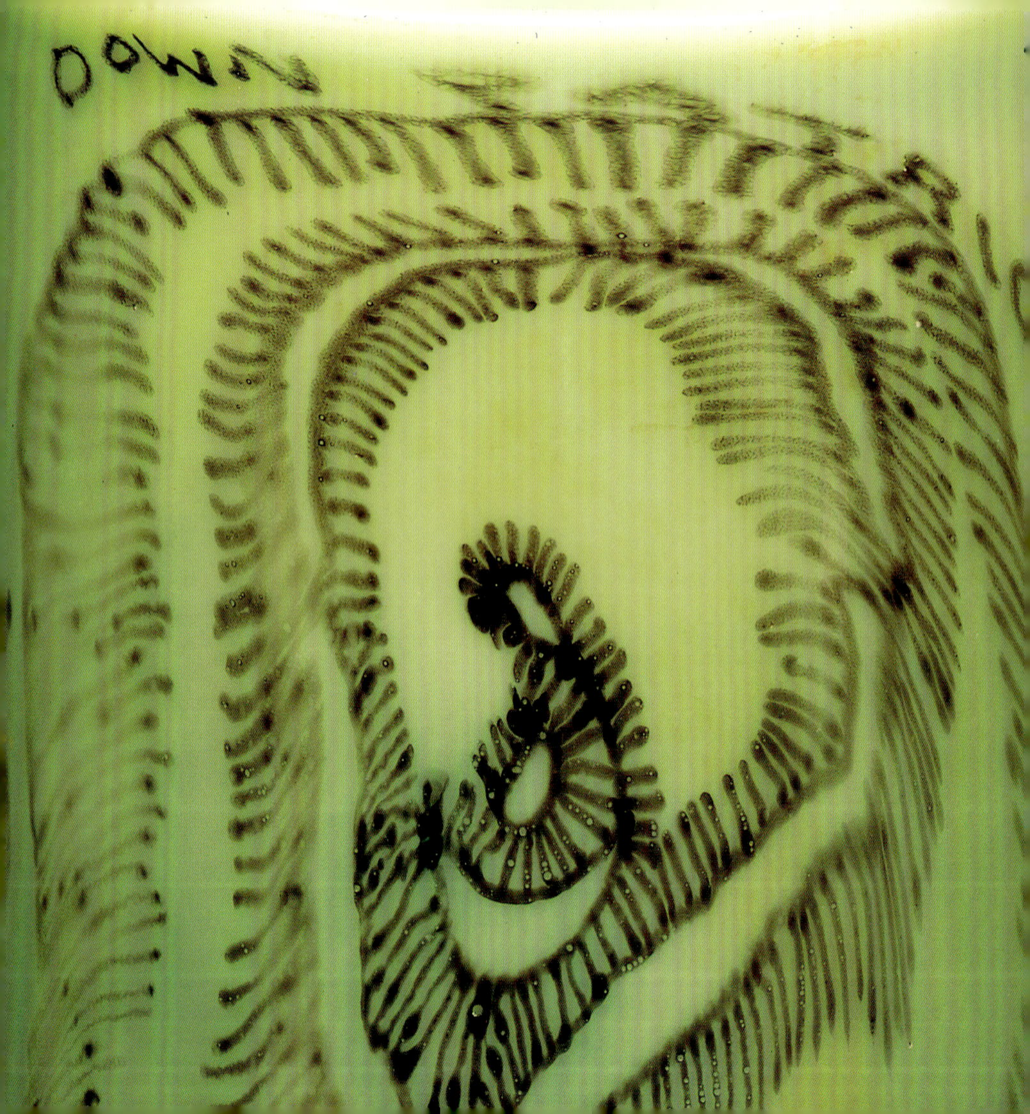

DOWN

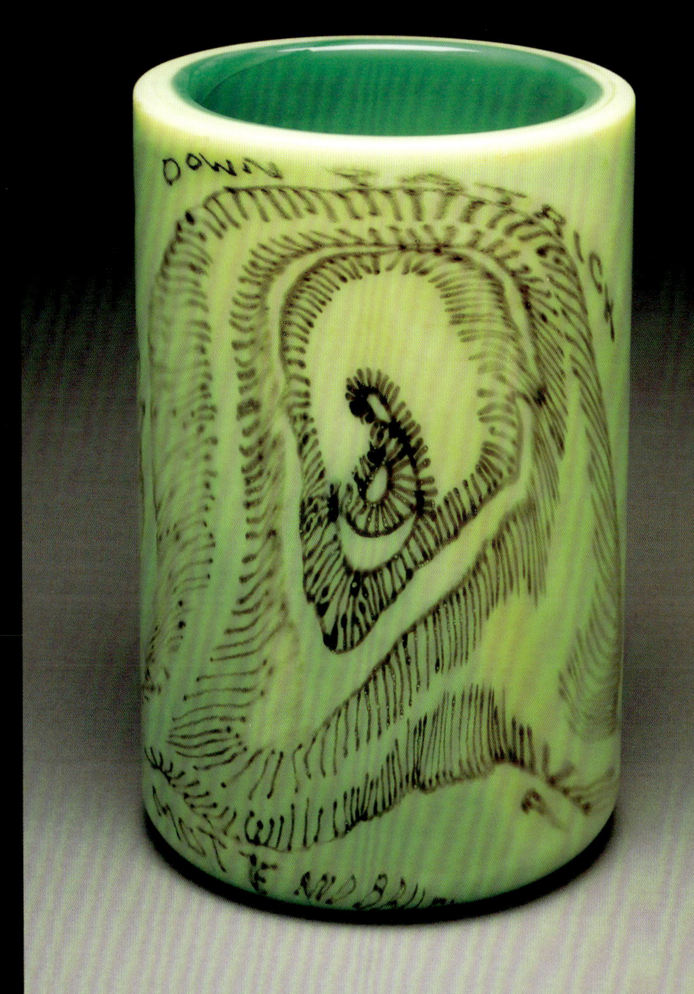

Irish Cylinder #5

In collaboration
with Seaver Leslie
1975, 12 x 8 x 8"

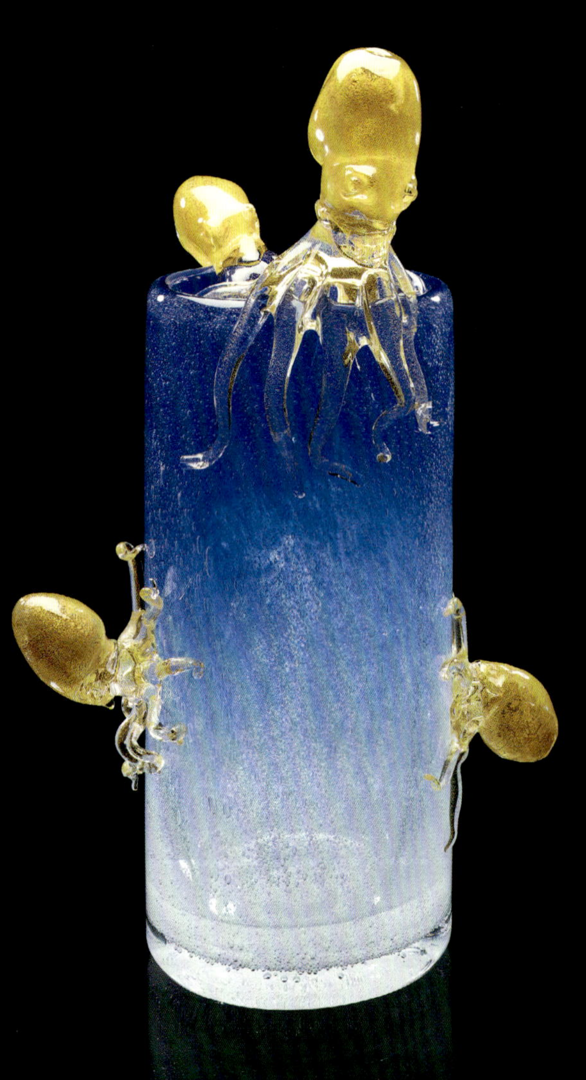

**Putti Sealife
Cylinder #1**

2000, 23 x 14 x 14"

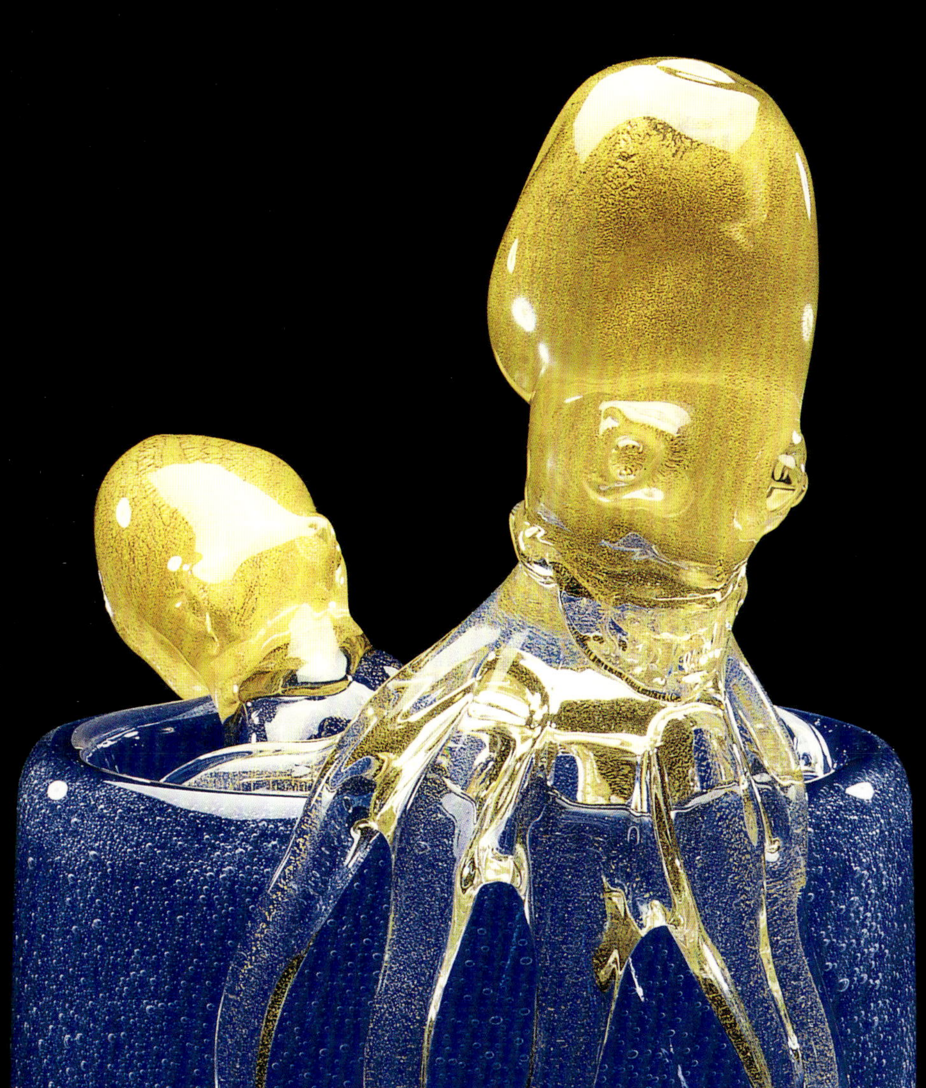

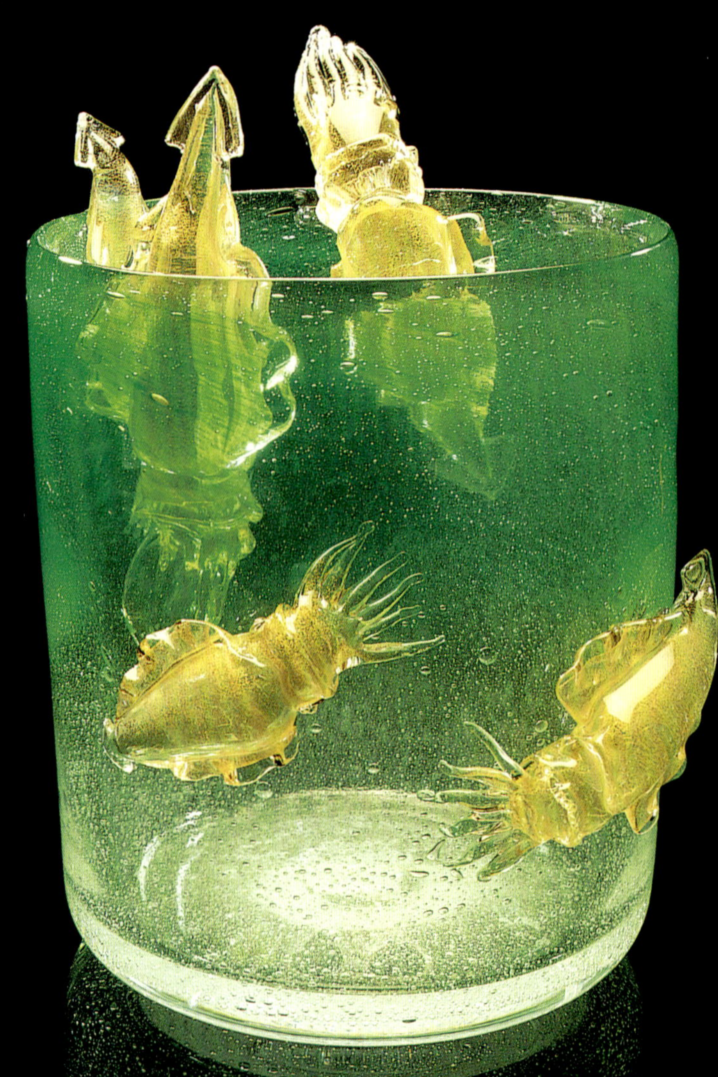

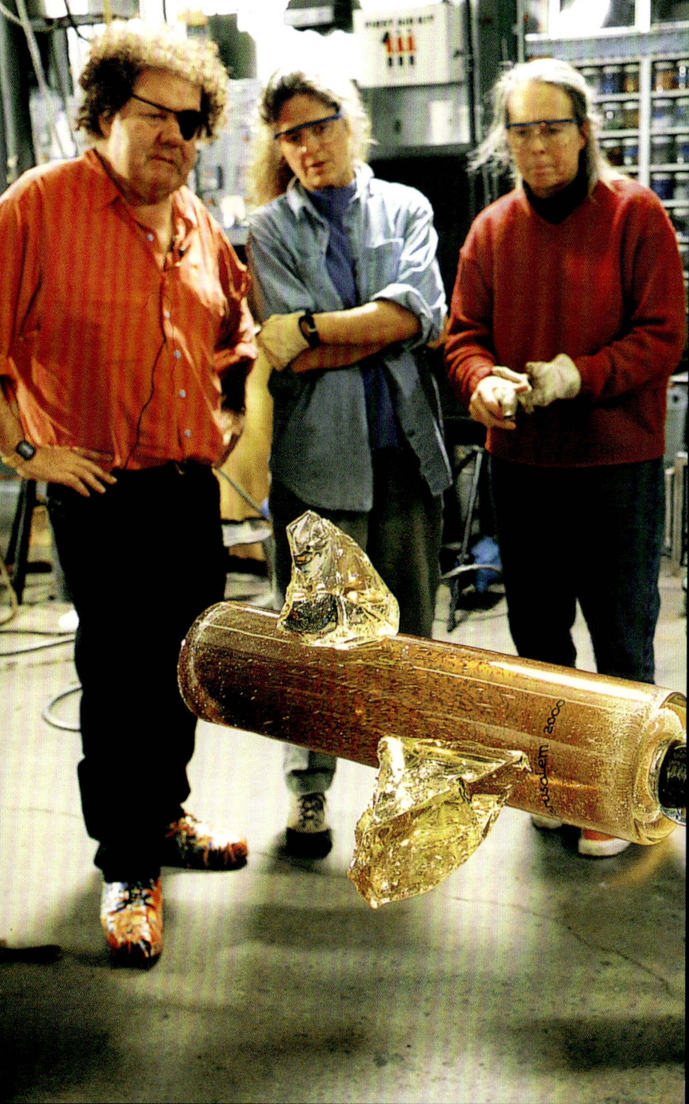

Putti Sealife
Cylinder #3

2000, 17 x 13 x 13"

Chihuly, Joey
Kirkpatrick, and
Flora C. Mace

The Boathouse hotshop
Seattle, Washington, 1999

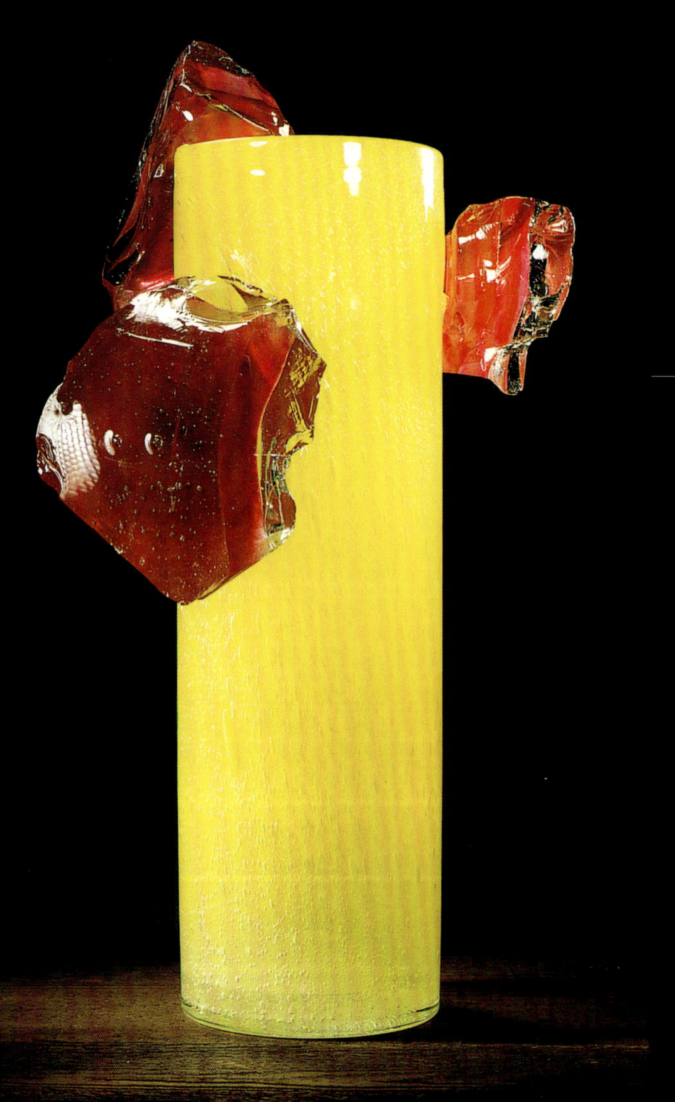

Jerusalem
Cylinder #119

1999, 27 x 15 x 16"

Jerusalem 2000
Cylinder #90

1999, 14 x 15 x 15"

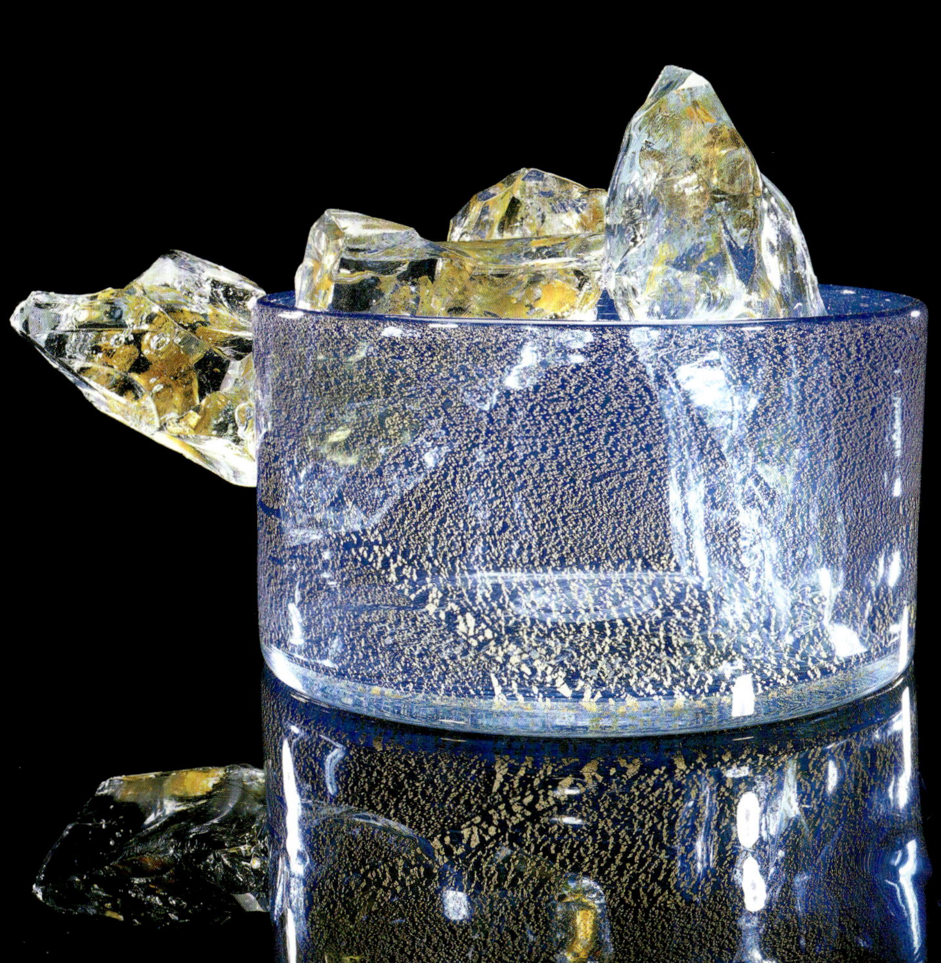

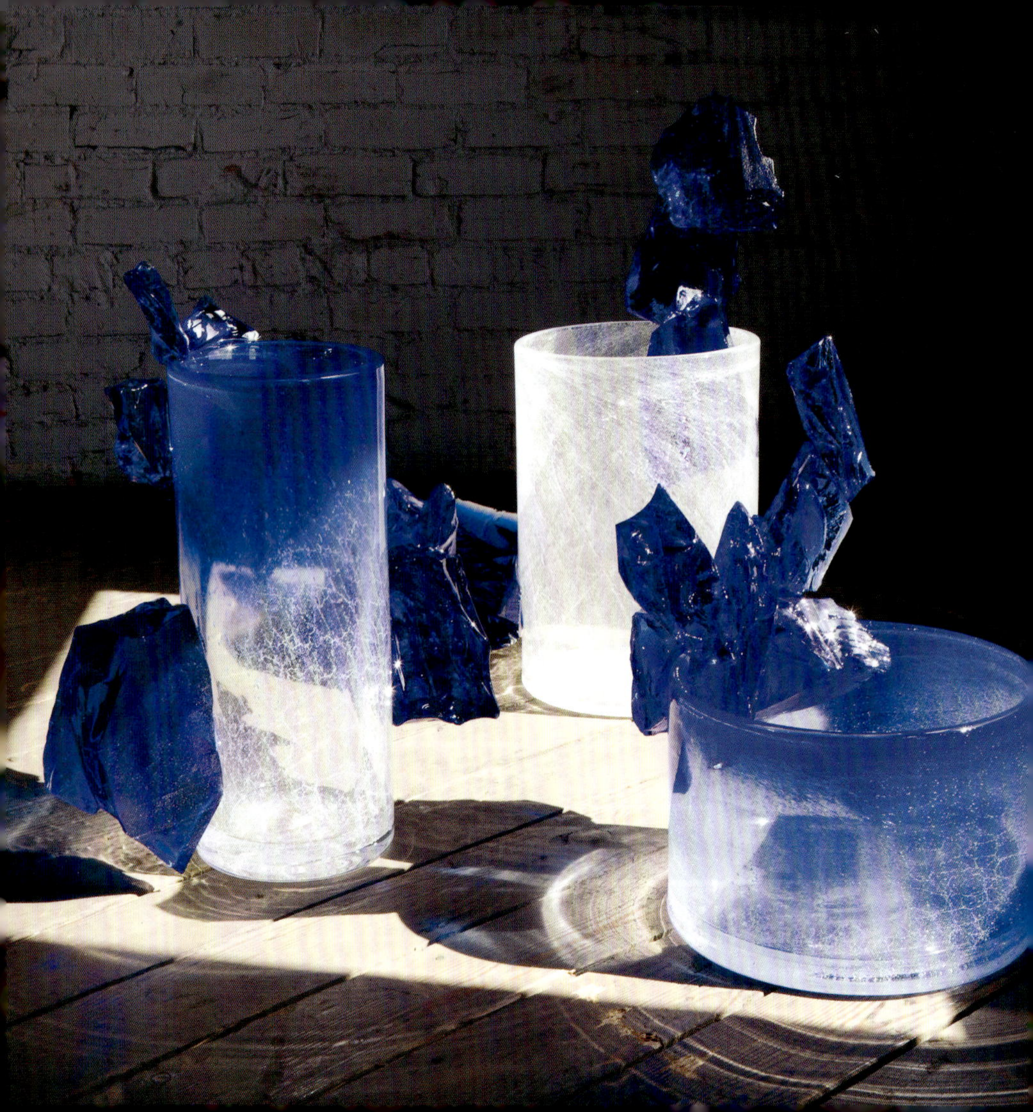

salem Cylinder Grouping

7

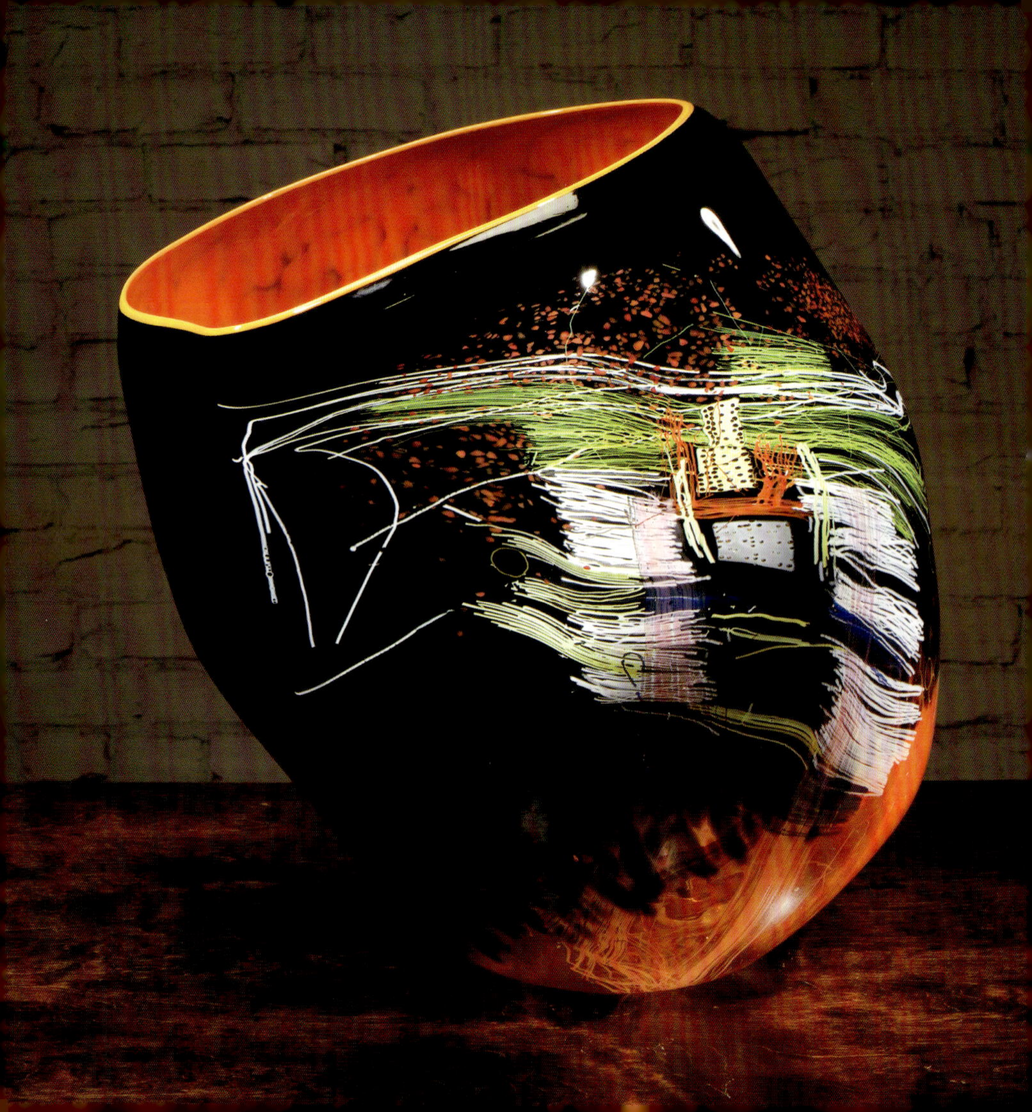

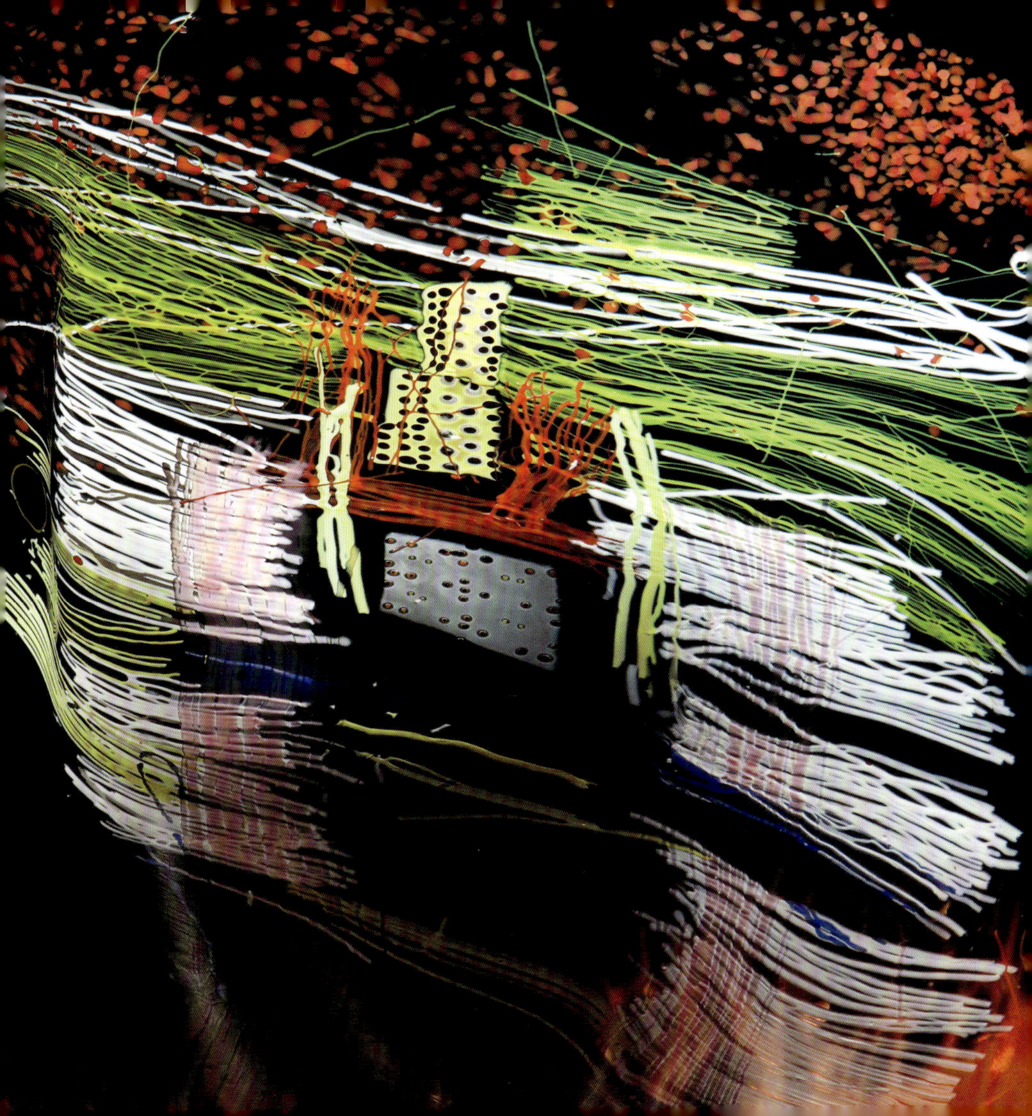

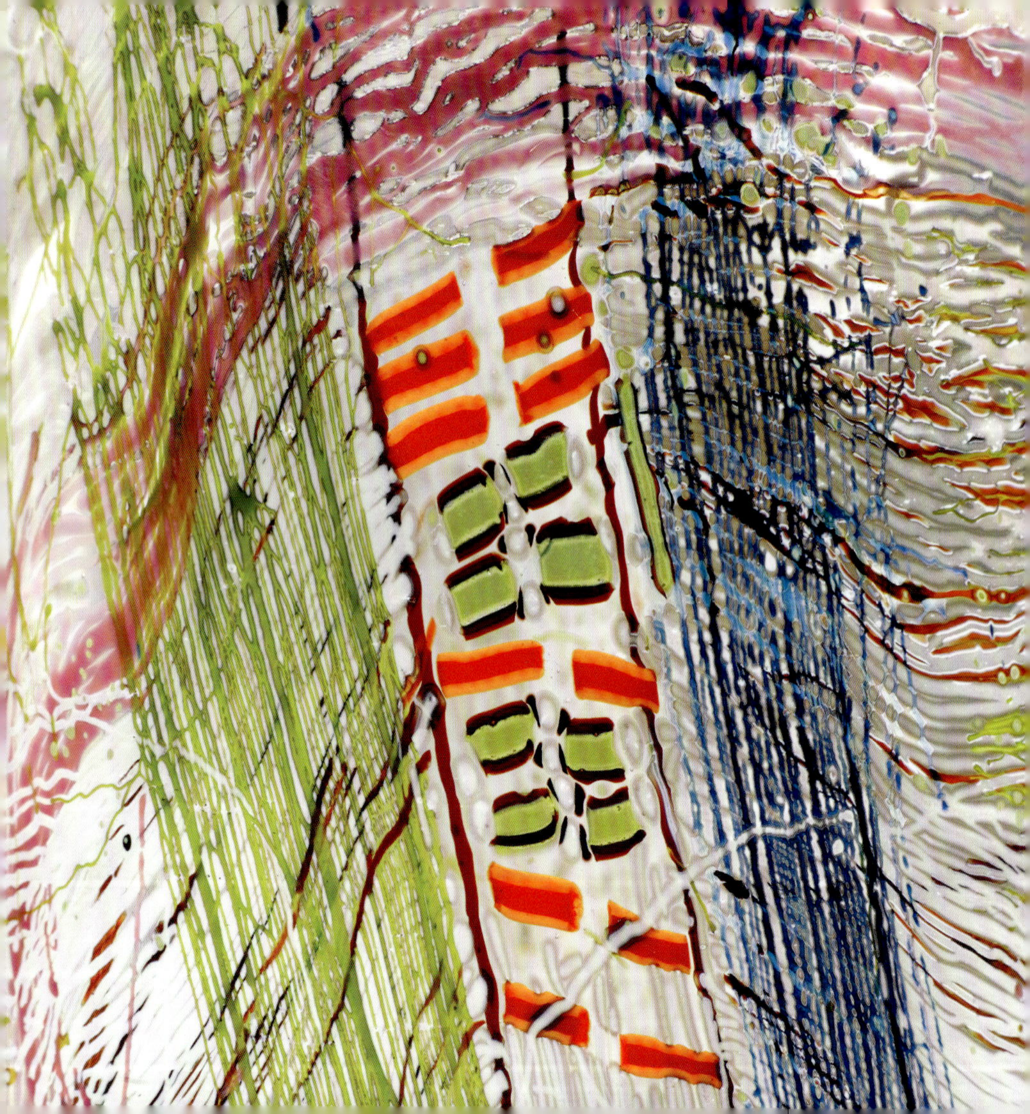

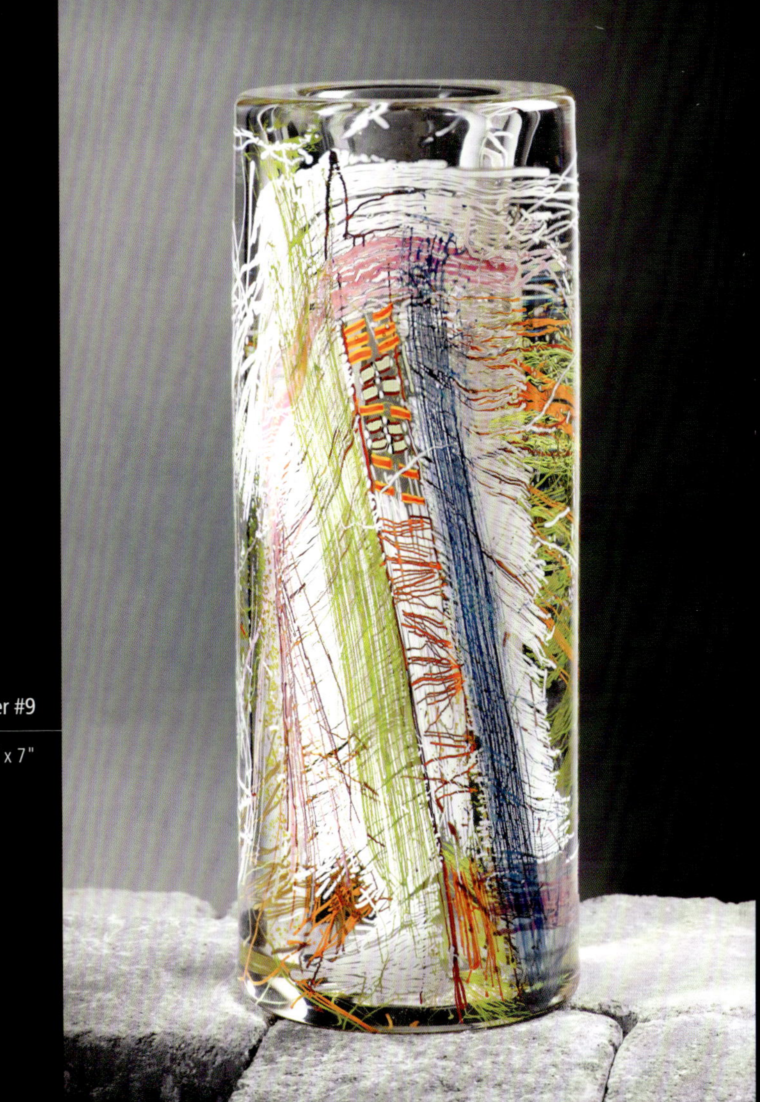

Clear Cylinder #9

2006, 18 x 7 x 7"

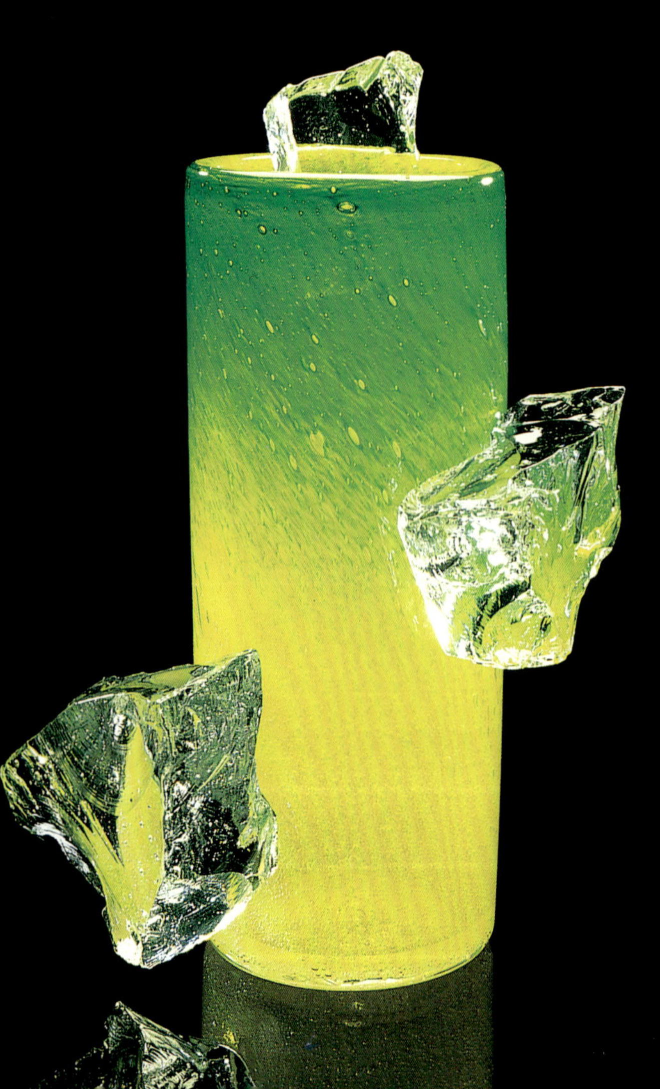

Jerusalem 2000
Cylinder

2000, 20 x 8 x 8"

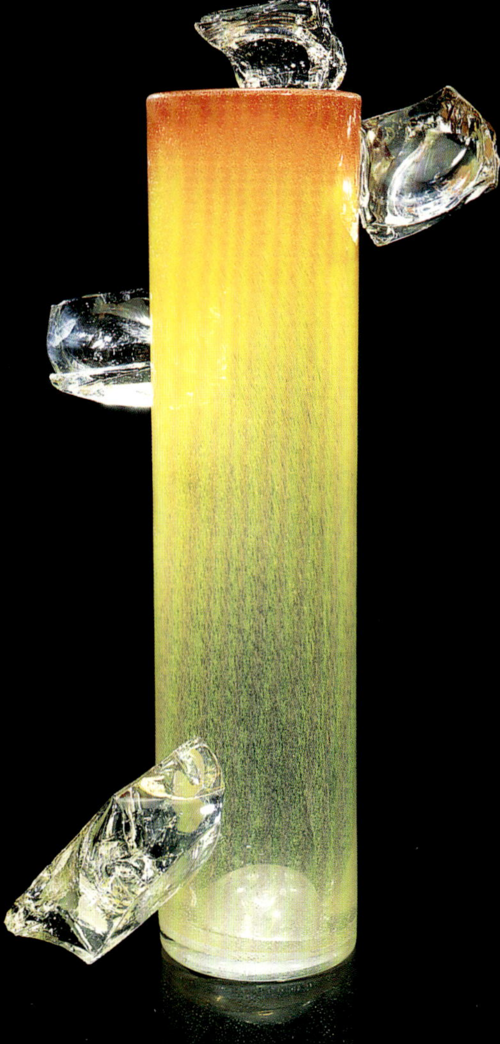

**Jerusalem 2000
Cylinder**

2001, 32 x 14 x 14"

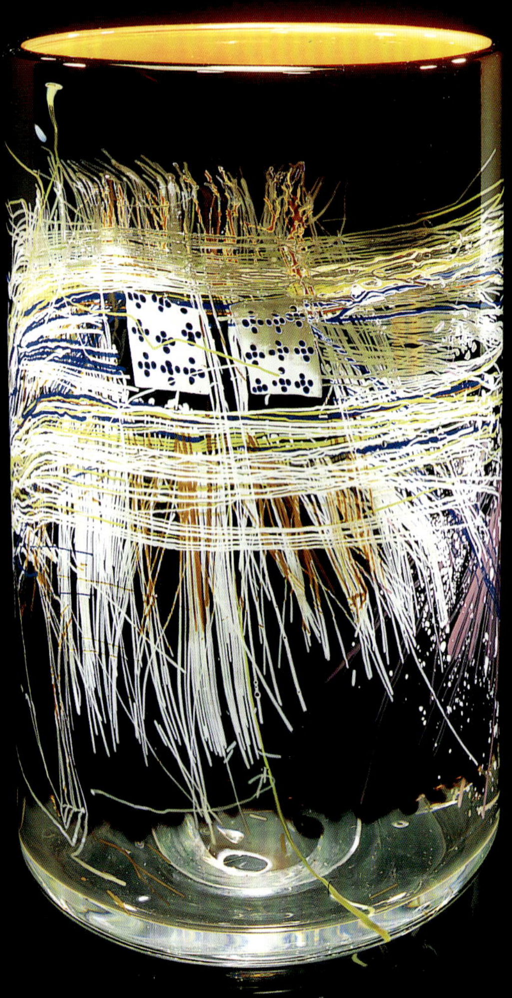

Black Cylinder #44

2006, 15 x 9 x 9"

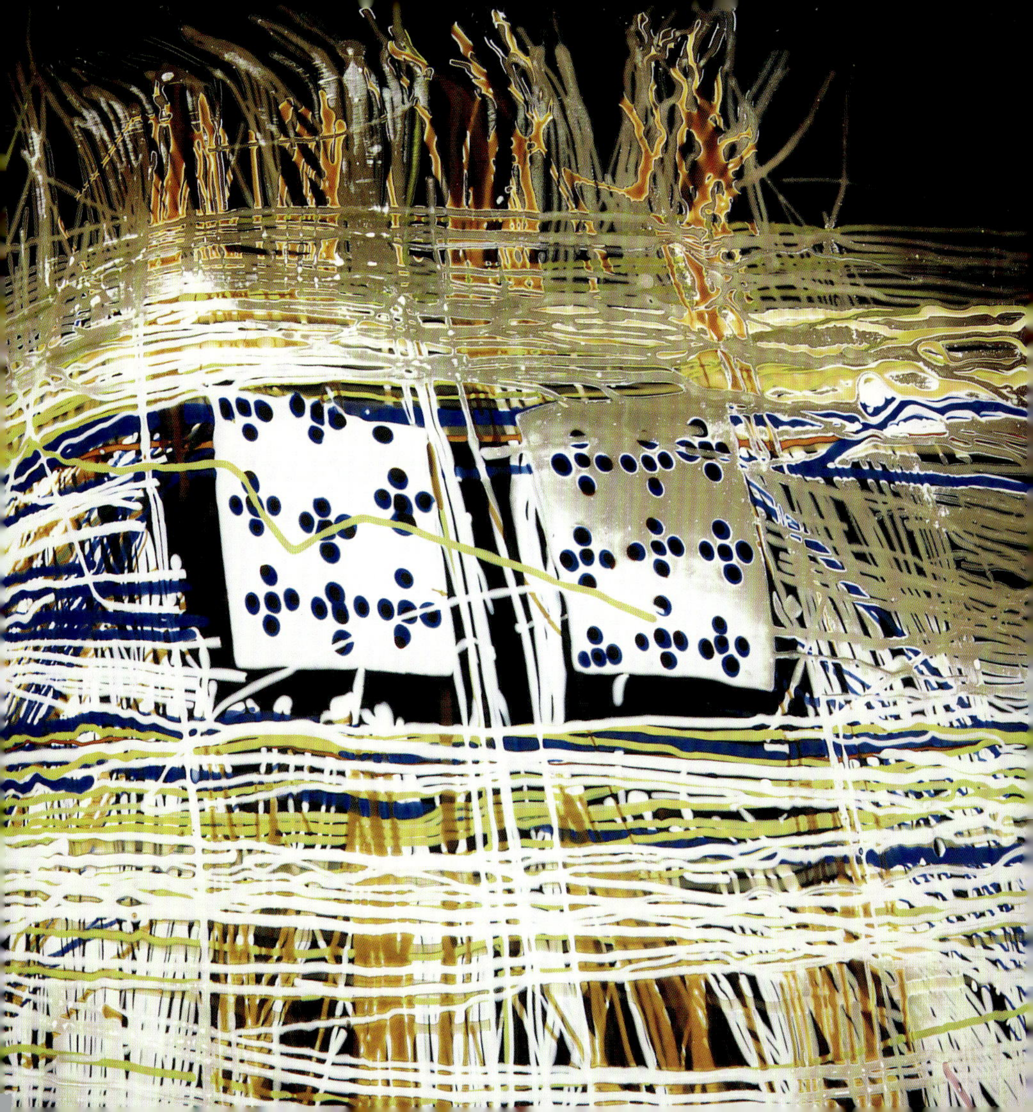

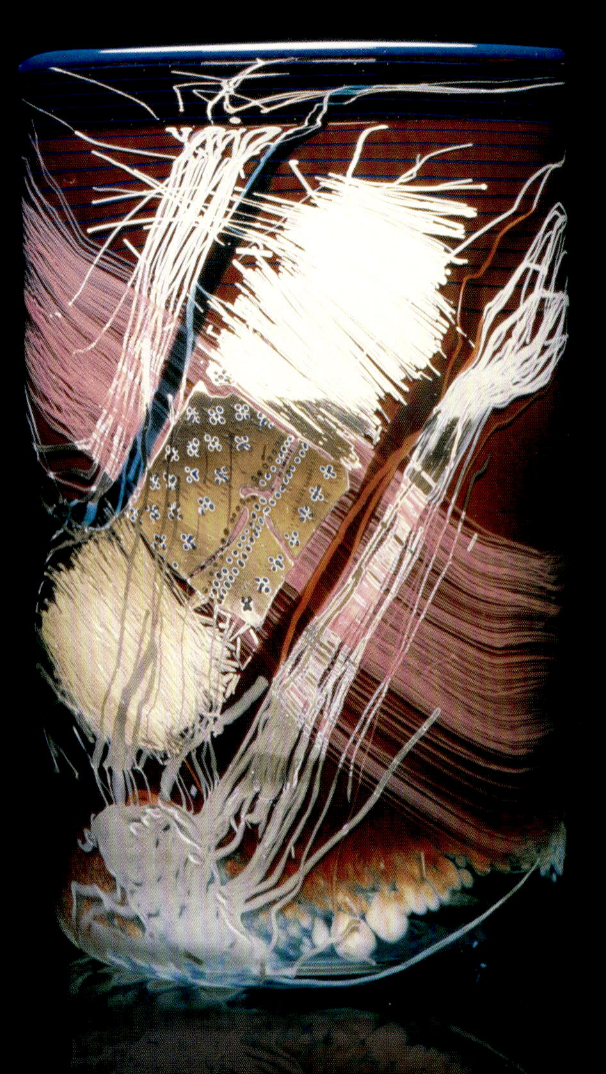

huck Cylinder

4, 15 x 7 x 7"

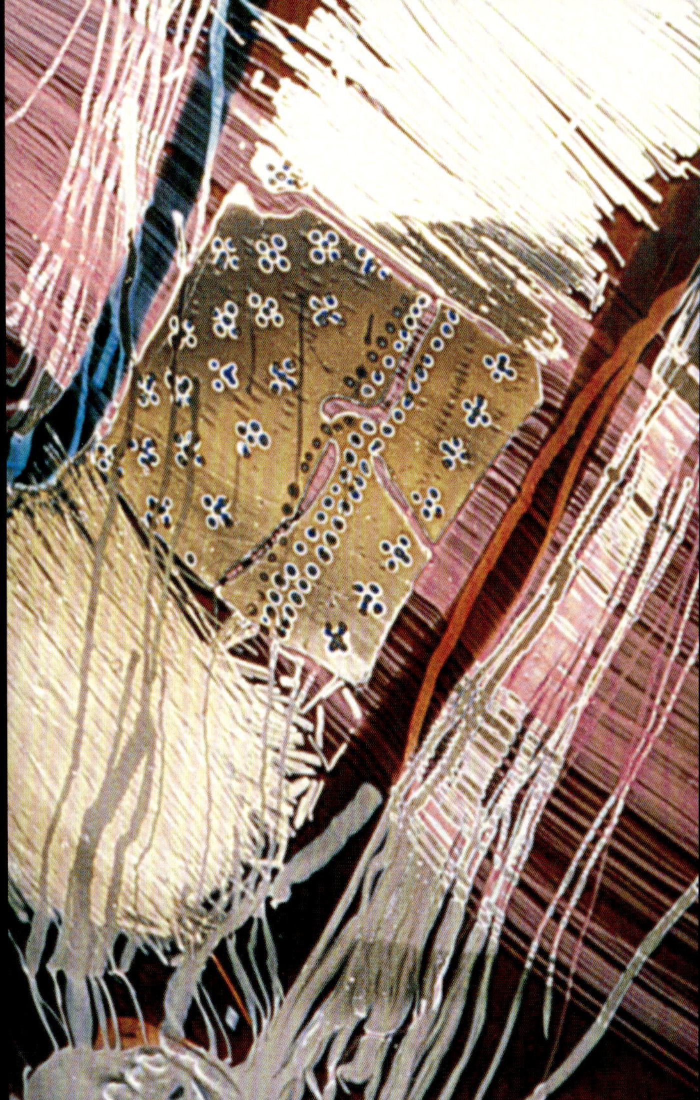

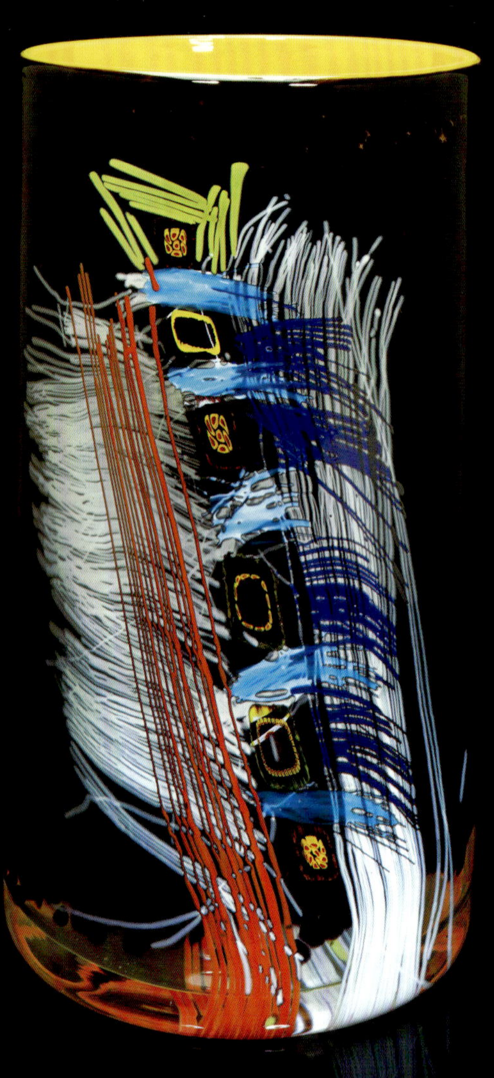

Black Cylinder #34

2006, 14 x 8 x 8"

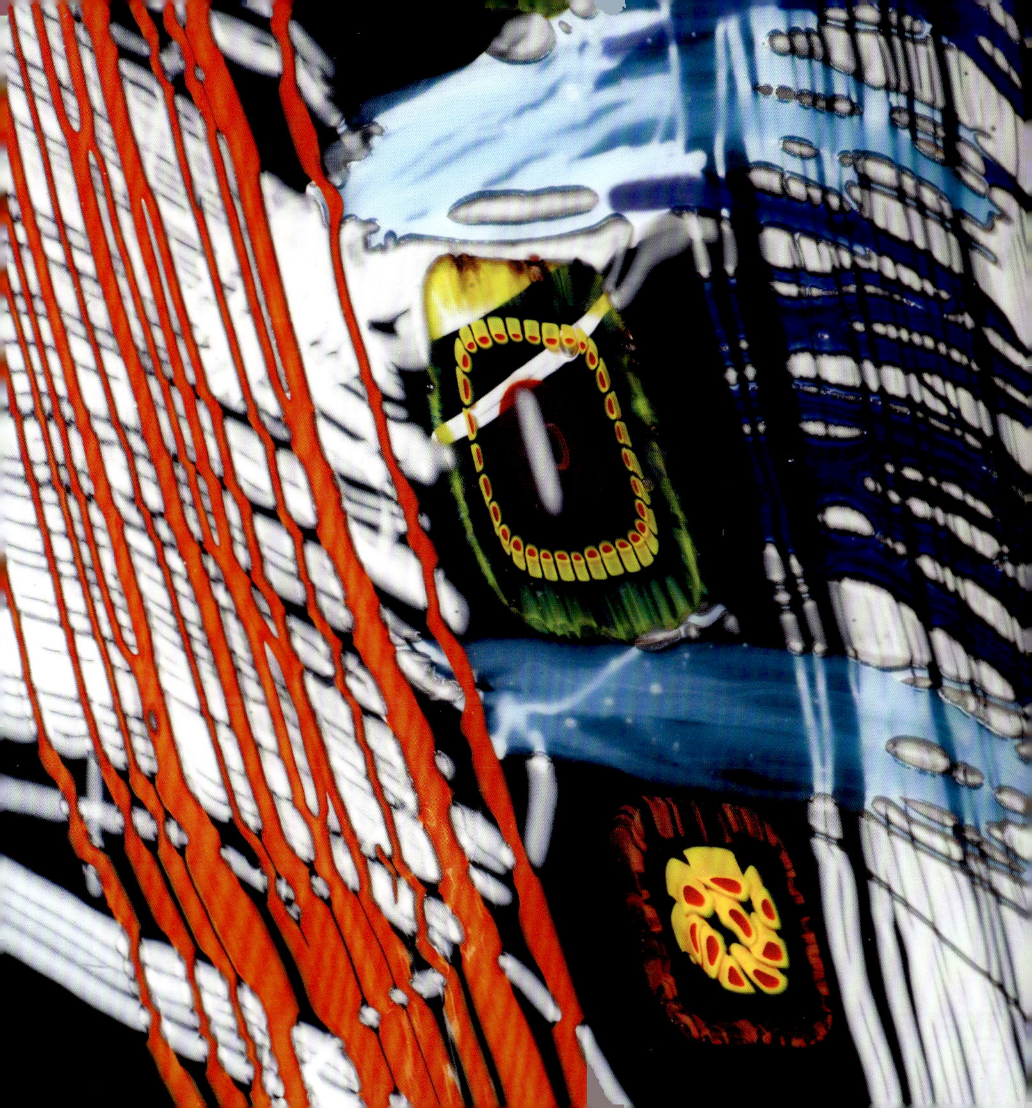

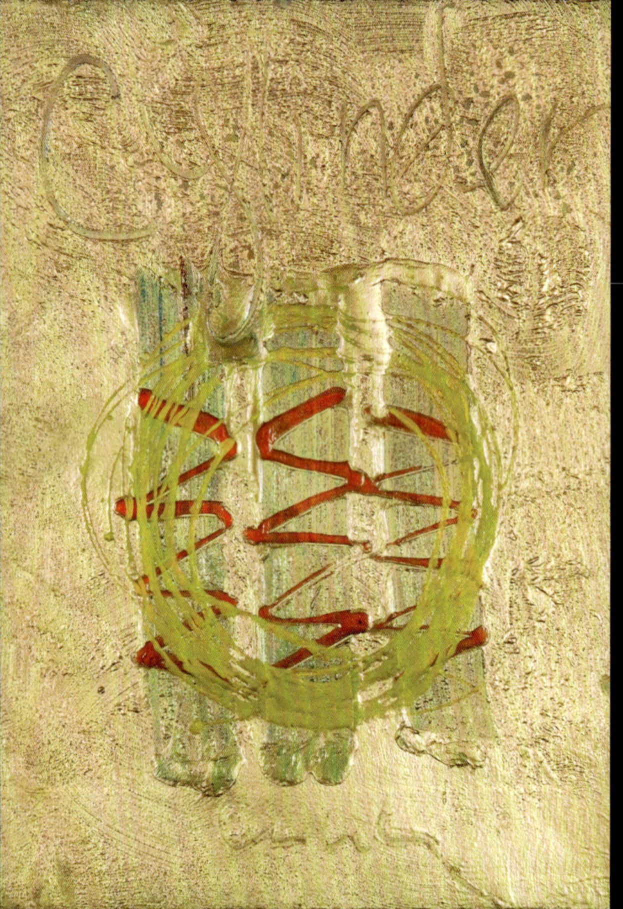

Antique Citron
Cylinder Drawing

2009, 30 x 22"

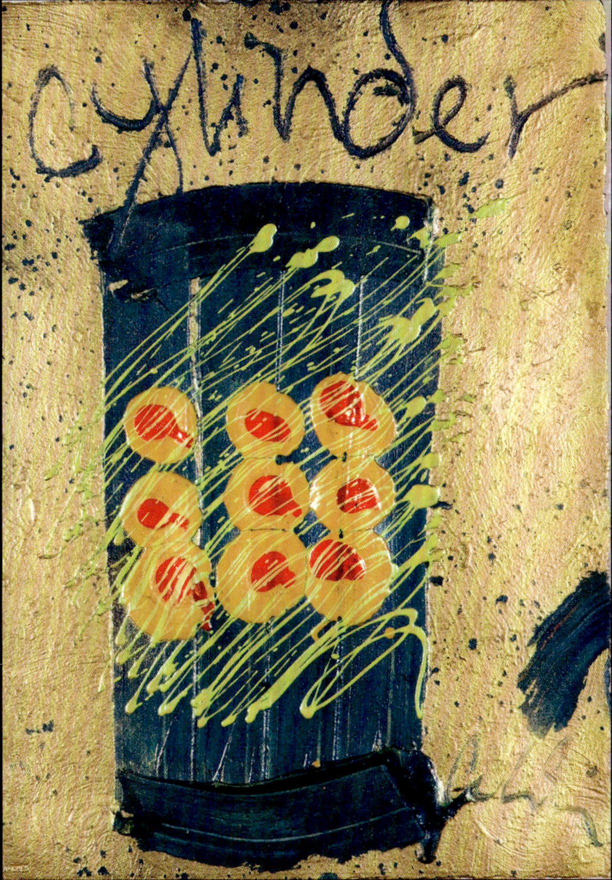

Steel Blue and Gilded
Ruby Cylinder Drawing

2009, 30 x 22"

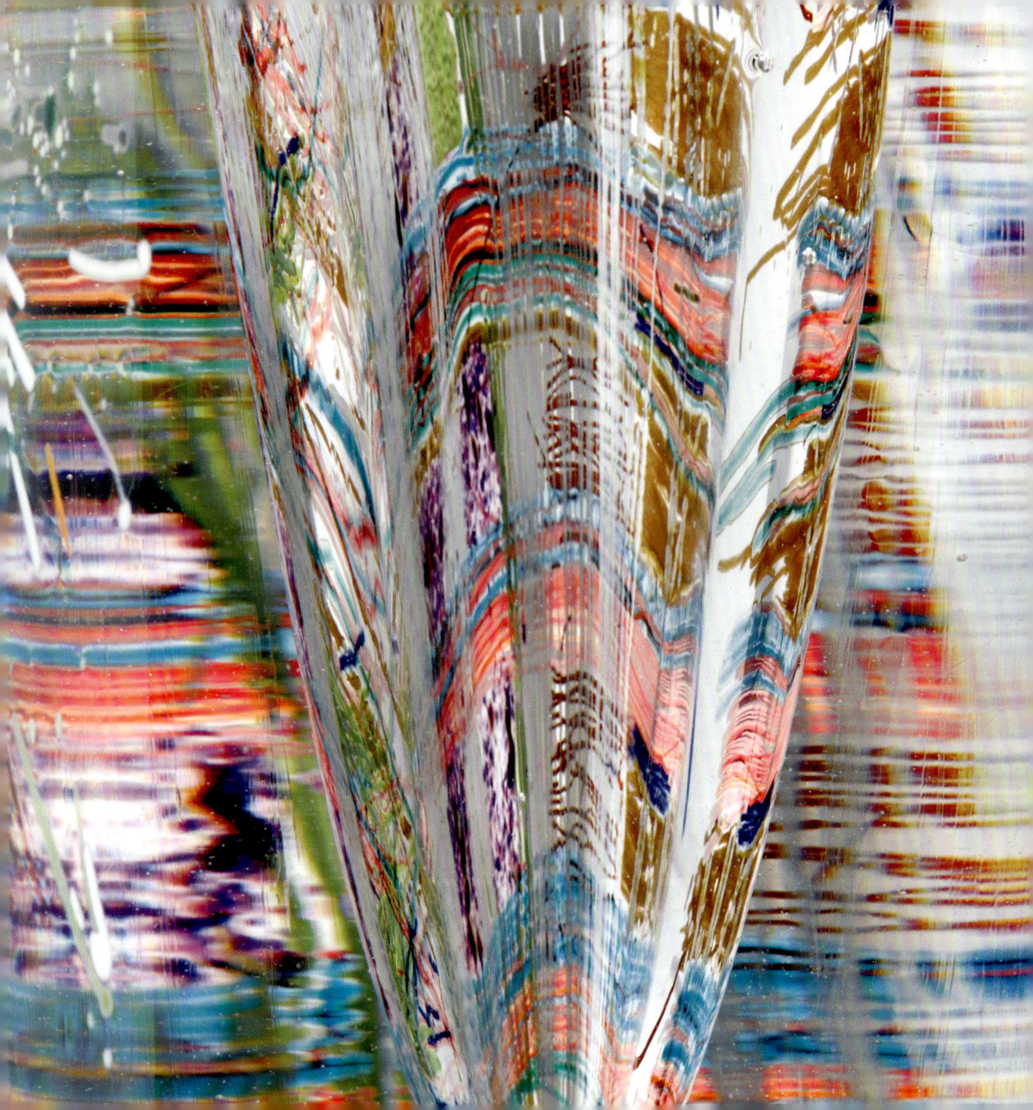

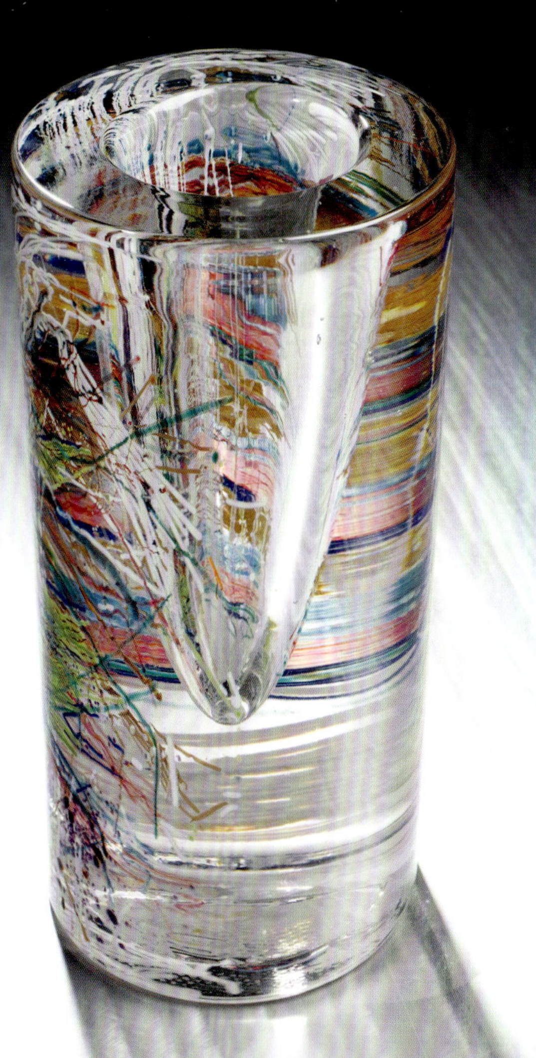

Clear Cylinder #5

2006, 16 x 8 x 8"

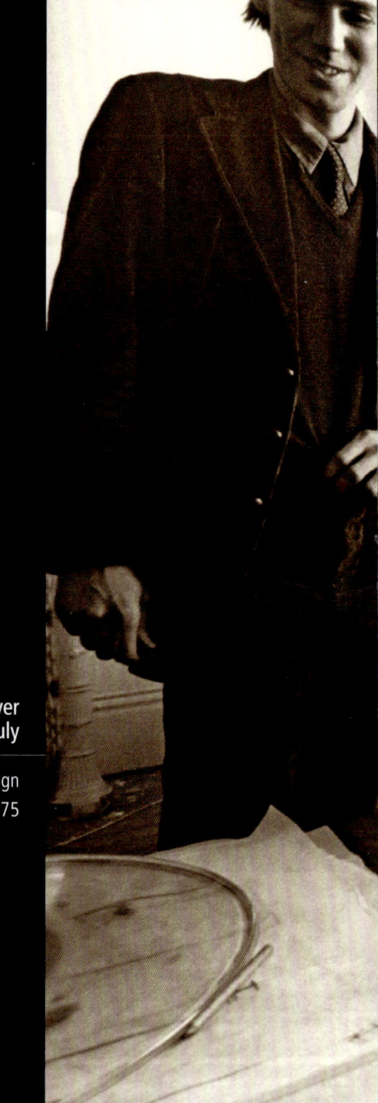

James Carpenter, Seaver
Leslie, and Chihuly

Rhode Island School of Design
Providence, Rhode Island, 1975

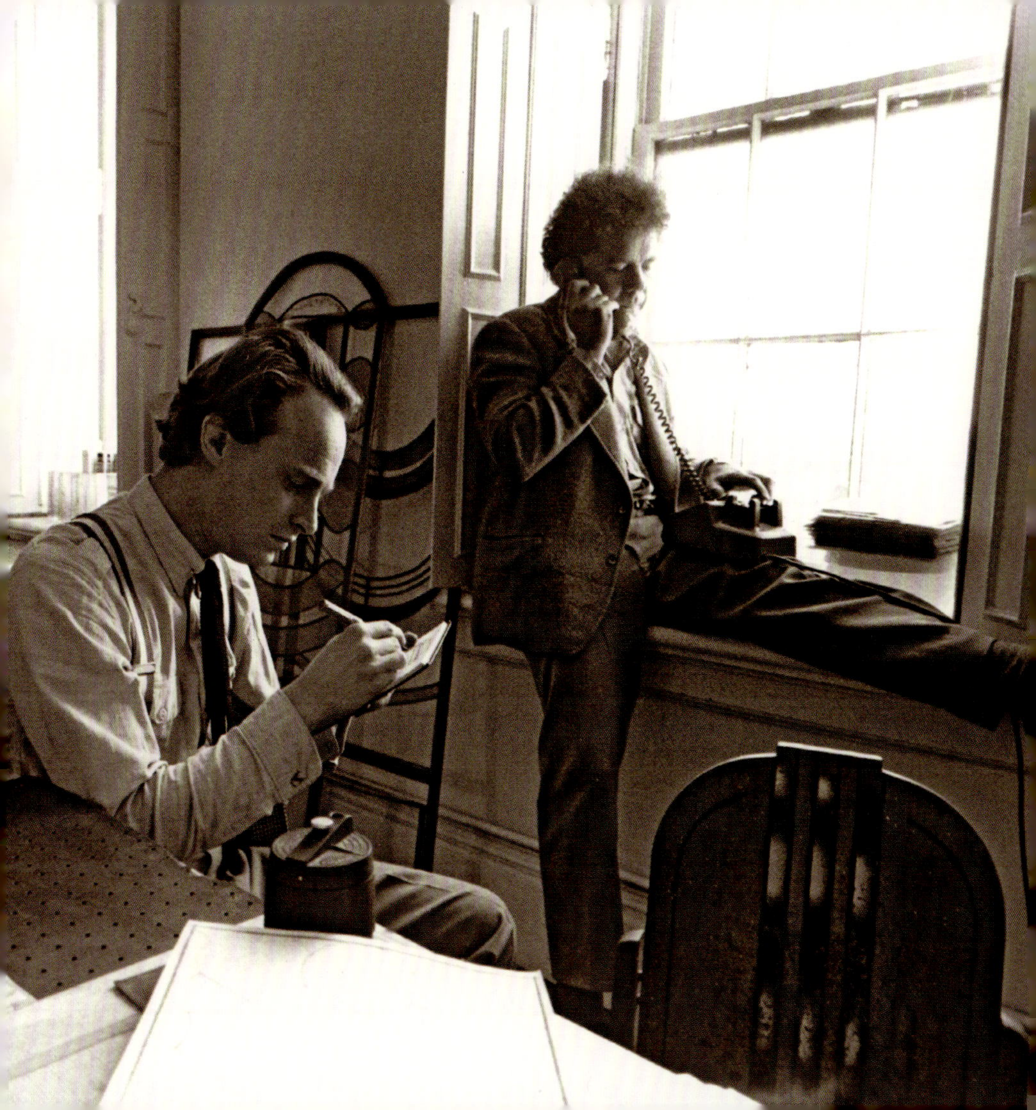

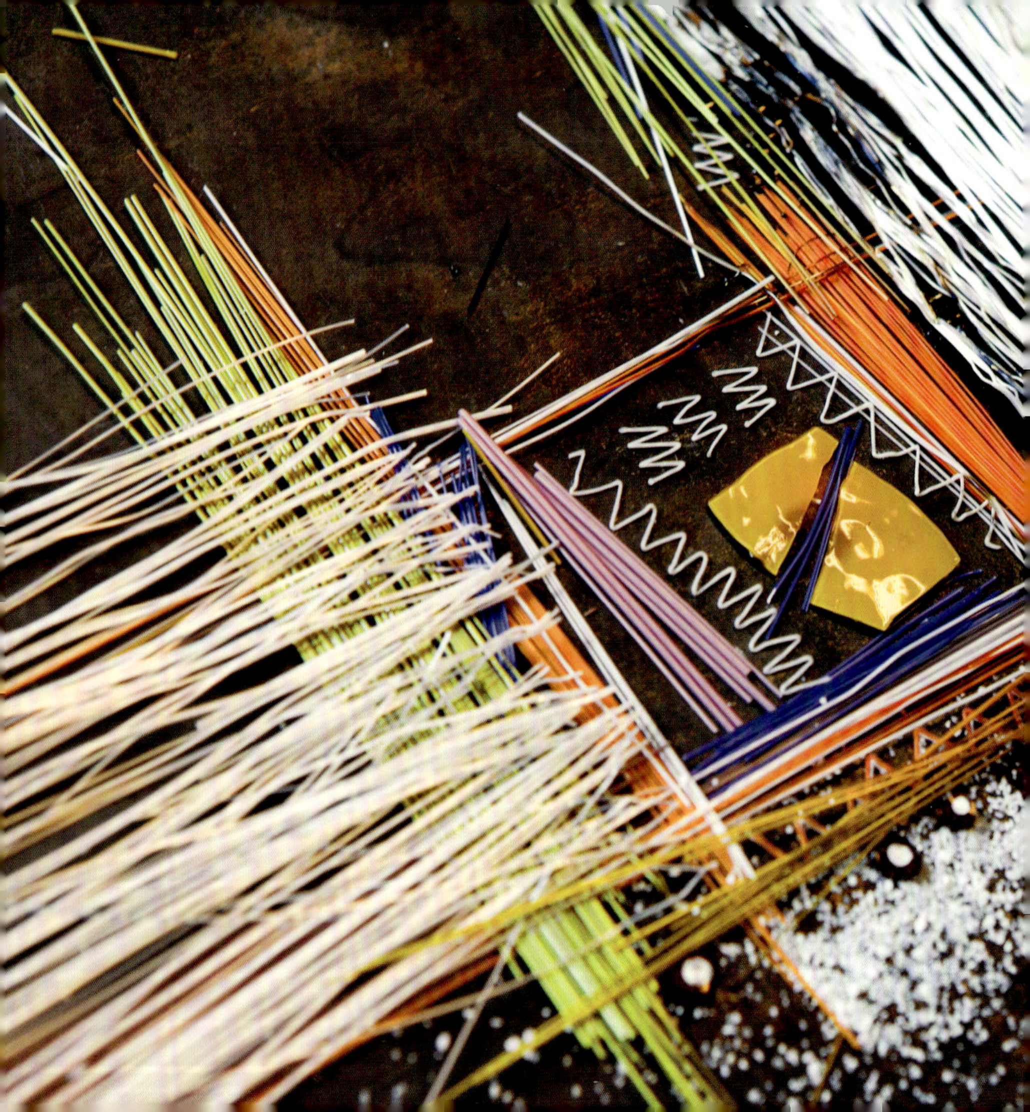

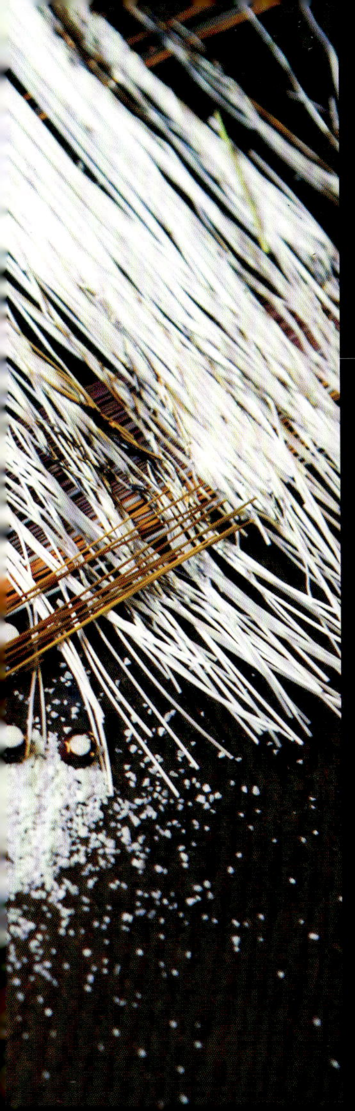

Cylinder shard drawing

The Boathouse hotshop
Seattle, Washington, 2006

Following page:
Jerusalem Cylinder in process

The Boathouse hotshop
Seattle, Washington, 1999

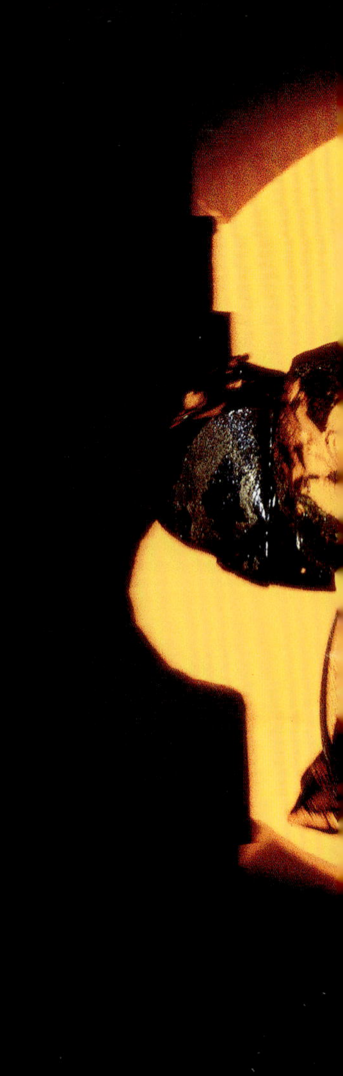

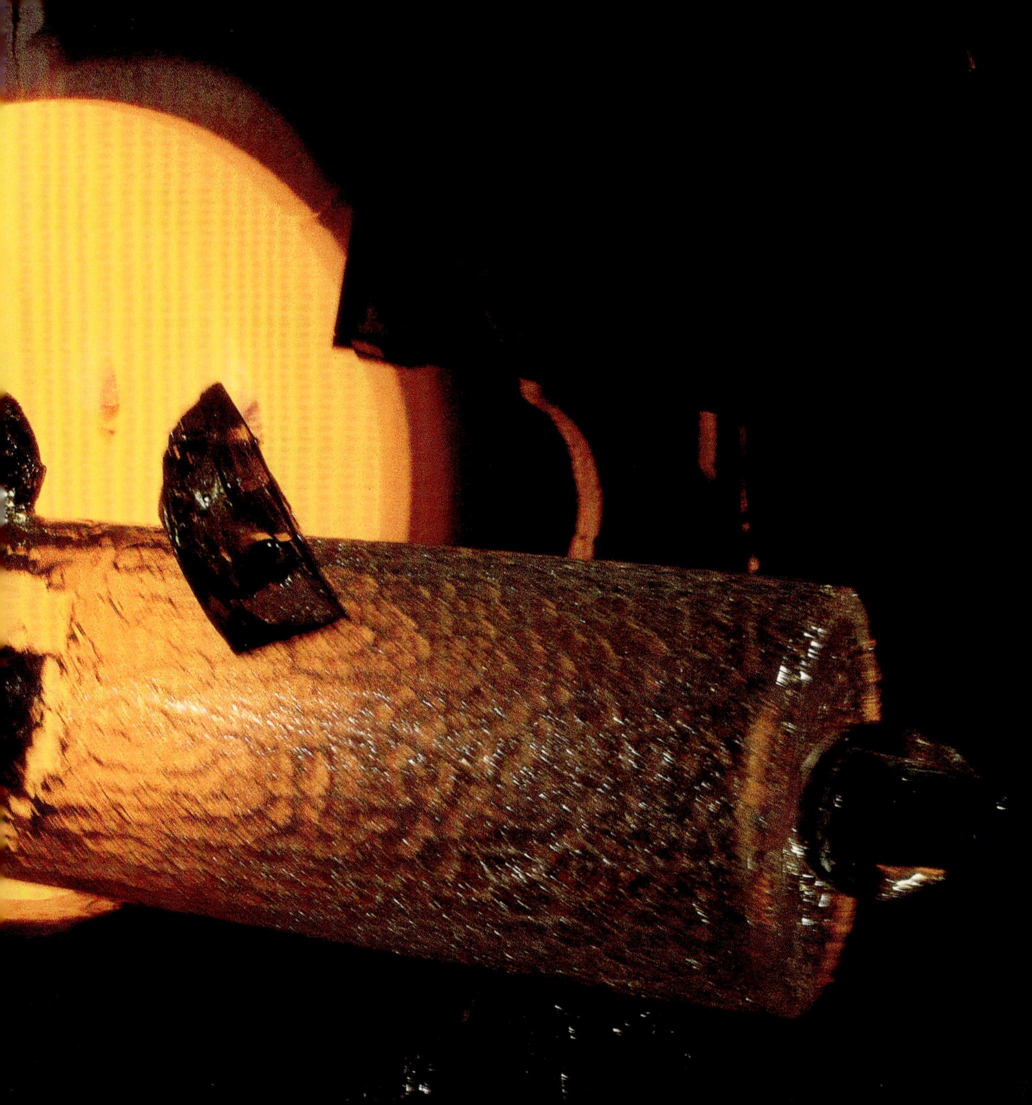

CHRONOLOGY

1941 Born September 20 in Tacoma, Washington, to George Chihuly and Viola Magnuson Chihuly.

1957 Older brother and only sibling, George, is killed in a Naval Air Force training accident in Pensacola, Florida.

1958 His father suffers a fatal heart attack at age 51. His mother goes to work to support Dale and herself.

1959 Graduates from high school in Tacoma. Enrolls in the College of Puget Sound (now the University of Puget Sound) in his hometown. Transfers to the University of Washington in Seattle to study interior design and architecture.

1961 Joins Delta Kappa Epsilon fraternity and becomes rush chairman. Learns to melt and fuse glass.

1962 Disillusioned with his studies, he leaves school and travels to Florence to study art. Discouraged by not being able to speak Italian, he leaves and travels to the Middle East.

1963 Works on a kibbutz in the Negev Desert. Returns to the University of Washington in the College of Arts and Sciences and studies under Hope Foote and Warren Hill. In a weaving class with Doris Brockway, he incorporates glass shards into woven tapestries.

1964 Returns to Europe, visits Leningrad, and makes the first of many trips to Ireland.

1965 Receives B.A. in Interior Design from the University of Washington. Experimenting on his own in his basement studio, Chihuly blows his first glass bubble by melting stained glass and using a metal pipe.

1966   Works as a commercial fisherman in Alaska to earn money for
        graduate school. Enters the University of Wisconsin at Madison,
        where he studies glassblowing under Harvey Littleton.

1967   Receives M.S. in Sculpture from the University of Wisconsin.
        Enrolls at the Rhode Island School of Design (RISD) in Providence,
        where he begins his exploration of environmental works using
        neon, argon, and blown glass. Awarded a Louis Comfort Tiffany
        Foundation Grant for work in glass. Italo Scanga, then on the
        faculty at Pennsylvania State University's Art Department, lec-
        tures at RISD, and the two begin a lifelong friendship.

1968   Receives M.F.A. in Ceramics from RISD. Awarded a Fulbright
        Fellowship, which enables him to travel and work in Europe.
        Becomes the first American glassblower to work in the Venini
        factory on the island of Murano. Returns to the United States and
        spends four consecutive summers teaching at Haystack Moun-
        tain School of Crafts in Deer Isle, Maine.

1969   Travels again throughout Europe and meets glass masters Erwin
        Eisch in Germany and Jaroslava Brychtová and Stanislav Libenský
        in Czechoslovakia. Returning to the United States, Chihuly estab-
        lishes the glass program at RISD, where he teaches for the next
        fifteen years.

1970   Meets James Carpenter, a student in the RISD Illustration
        Department, and they begin a four-year collaboration.

1971   On the site of a tree farm owned by Seattle art patrons Anne
        Gould Hauberg and John Hauberg, the Pilchuck Glass School

experiment is started. Chihuly's first environmental installation at Pilchuck is created that summer. He resumes teaching at RISD and creates *20,000 Pounds of Ice and Neon, Glass Forest #1,* and *Glass Forest #2* with James Carpenter, installations that prefigure later environmental works by Chihuly.

1972   Continues to collaborate with Carpenter on large-scale architectural projects. They create *Rondel Door* and *Cast Glass Door* at Pilchuck. Back in Providence, they create *Dry Ice, Bent Glass and Neon,* a conceptual breakthrough.

1974   Supported by a National Endowment for the Arts grant at Pilchuck, James Carpenter, a group of students, and he develop a technique for picking up glass thread drawings. In December at RISD, he completes his last collaborative project with Carpenter, *Corning Wall.*

1975   At RISD, begins series of *Navajo Blanket Cylinders.* Kate Elliott and, later, Flora C. Mace fabricate the complex thread drawings. He receives the first of two National Endowment for the Arts Individual Artist grants. Artist-in-residence with Seaver Leslie at Artpark, on the Niagara Gorge, in New York State. Begins *Irish Cylinders* and *Ulysses Cylinders* with Leslie and Mace.

1976   An automobile accident in England leaves him, after weeks in the hospital and 256 stitches in his face, without sight in his left eye and with permanent damage to his right ankle and foot. After recuperating he returns to Providence to serve as head of the Department of Sculpture and the Program in Glass at RISD.

Henry Geldzahler, curator of contemporary art at the Metropolitan Museum of Art in New York, acquires three *Navajo Blanket Cylinders* for the museum's collection. This is a turning point in Chihuly's career, and a friendship between artist and curator commences.

1977   Inspired by Northwest Coast Indian baskets he sees at the Washington State Historical Society in Tacoma, begins the *Basket* series at Pilchuck over the summer, with Benjamin Moore as his gaffer. Continues his bicoastal teaching assignments, dividing his time between Rhode Island and the Pacific Northwest.

1978   Meets William Morris, a student at Pilchuck Glass School, and the two begin a close, eight-year working relationship. A solo show curated by Michael W. Monroe at the Renwick Gallery, Smithsonian Institution, in Washington, D.C., is another career milestone.

1979   Dislocates his shoulder in a bodysurfing accident and relinquishes the gaffer position for good. William Morris becomes his chief gaffer for the next several years. Chihuly begins to make drawings as a way to communicate his designs.

1980   Resigns his teaching position at RISD. He returns there periodically during the 1980s as artist-in-residence. Begins *Seaform* series at Pilchuck in the summer and later, back in Providence, returns to architectural installations with the creation of windows for the Shaare Emeth Synagogue in St. Louis, Missouri.

1981   Begins *Macchia* series.

1982   First major catalog is published: *Chihuly Glass*, designed by RISD colleague and friend Malcolm Grear.

1983   Returns to the Pacific Northwest after sixteen years on the East Coast. Works at Pilchuck in the fall and winter, further developing the *Macchia* series with William Morris as chief gaffer.

1984   Begins work on the *Soft Cylinder* series, with Flora C. Mace and Joey Kirkpatrick executing the glass drawings.

1985   Begins working hot glass on a larger scale and creates several site-specific installations.

1986   Begins *Persian* series with Martin Blank as gaffer, assisted by Robbie Miller. With the opening of *Objets de Verre* at the Musée des Arts Décoratifs, Palais du Louvre, in Paris, he becomes one of only four American artists to have had a one-person exhibition at the Louvre.

1987   Establishes his first hotshop in the Van de Kamp Building near Lake Union, Seattle. Begins association with artist Parks Anderson. Marries playwright Sylvia Peto.

1988   Inspired by a private collection of Italian Art Deco glass, Chihuly begins *Venetian* series. Working from Chihuly's drawings, Lino Tagliapietra serves as gaffer.

1989   With Italian glass masters Lino Tagliapietra, Pino Signoretto, and a team of glassblowers at Pilchuck Glass School, begins *Putti* series. Working with Tagliapietra, Chihuly creates *Ikebana* series, inspired by his travels to Japan and exposure to ikebana masters.

1990   Purchases the historic Pocock Building located on Lake Union, realizing his dream of being on the water in Seattle. Renovates the building and names it The Boathouse, for use as a studio, hotshop, and archives. Travels to Japan.

1991   Begins *Niijima Float* series with Richard Royal as gaffer, creating some of the largest pieces of glass ever blown by hand. Completes a number of architectural installations. He and Sylvia Peto divorce.

1992   Begins *Chandelier* series with a hanging sculpture at the Seattle Art Museum. Designs sets for Seattle Opera production of Debussy's *Pelléas et Mélisande*.

1993   Begins *Piccolo Venetian* series with Lino Tagliapietra. Creates *100,000 Pounds of Ice and Neon*, a temporary installation in the Tacoma Dome, Tacoma, Washington.

1994   Creates five installations for Tacoma's Union Station Federal Courthouse. Hilltop Artists in Residence, a glassblowing program for at-risk youths in Tacoma, Washington, is created by friend Kathy Kaperick. Within two years the program partners with Tacoma Public Schools, and Chihuly remains a strong role model and adviser.

1995   *Chihuly Over Venice* begins with a glassblowing session in Nuutajärvi, Finland, and a subsequent blow at the Waterford Crystal factory, Ireland.

1996   *Chihuly Over Venice* continues with a blow in Monterrey, Mexico, and culminates with the installation of fourteen

Chandeliers at various sites in Venice. Creates his first permanent outdoor installation, *Icicle Creek Chandelier.*

1997   Continues and expands series of experimental plastics he calls "Polyvitro." *Chihuly* is designed by Massimo Vignelli and copublished by Harry N. Abrams, Inc., New York, and Portland Press, Seattle. A permanent installation of Chihuly's work opens at the Hakone Glass Forest, Ukai Museum, in Hakone, Japan.

1998   Chihuly is invited to Sydney, Australia, with his team to participate in the Sydney Arts Festival. A son, Jackson Viola Chihuly, is born February 12 to Dale Chihuly and Leslie Jackson. Creates architectural installations for Benaroya Hall, Seattle; Bellagio, Las Vegas; and Atlantis, the Bahamas.

1999   Begins *Jerusalem Cylinder* series with gaffer James Mongrain in concert with Flora C. Mace and Joey Kirkpatrick. Mounts his most challenging exhibition: *Chihuly in the Light of Jerusalem 2000*, at the Tower of David Museum of the History of Jerusalem. Outside the museum he creates a sixty-foot wall from twenty-four massive blocks of ice shipped from Alaska.

2000   Creates *La Tour de Lumière* sculpture as part of the exhibition *Contemporary American Sculpture* in Monte Carlo. Marlborough gallery represents Chihuly. More than a million visitors enter the Tower of David Museum to see *Chihuly in the Light of Jerusalem 2000*, breaking the world attendance record for a temporary exhibition during 1999–2000.

2001   *Chihuly at the V&A* opens at the Victoria and Albert

Museum in London. Exhibits at Marlborough Gallery, New York and London. Groups a series of *Chandeliers* for the first time to create an installation for the Mayo Clinic in Rochester, Minnesota. Artist Italo Scanga dies, friend and mentor for over three decades. Presents his first major glasshouse exhibition, *Chihuly in the Park: A Garden of Glass*, at the Garfield Park Conservatory, Chicago.

2002   Creates installations for the Salt Lake 2002 Olympic Winter Games. The *Chihuly Bridge of Glass*, conceived by Chihuly and designed in collaboration with Arthur Andersson of Andersson·Wise Architects, is dedicated in Tacoma, Washington.

2003   Begins the *Fiori* series with gaffer Joey DeCamp for the opening exhibition at the Tacoma Art Museum's new building. TAM designs a permanent installation for its collection of his works. *Chihuly at the Conservatory* opens at the Franklin Park Conservatory, Columbus, Ohio.

2004   Creates new forms in his *Fiori* series for an exhibition at Marlborough Gallery, New York. The Orlando Museum of Art and the Museum of Fine Arts, St. Petersburg, Florida, become the first museums to collaborate and present simultaneous major exhibitions of his work. Presents a glasshouse exhibition at Atlanta Botanical Garden.

2005   Marries Leslie Jackson. Mounts a major garden exhibition at the Royal Botanic Gardens, Kew, outside London. Shows at Marlborough Monaco and Marlborough London. Exhibits at the Fairchild Tropical Botanic Garden, Coral Gables, Florida.

2006   Mother, Viola, dies at the age of ninety-eight in Tacoma, Washington. Begins *Black* series with a *Cylinder* blow. Presents glasshouse exhibitions at the Missouri Botanical Garden and the New York Botanical Garden. *Chihuly in Tacoma*—hotshop sessions at the Museum of Glass—reunites Chihuly and glassblowers from important periods in his artistic development. The film *Chihuly in the Hotshop* documents this event.

2007   Exhibits at the Phipps Conservatory and Botanical Gardens, Pittsburgh. Creates stage sets for the Seattle Symphony's production of Béla Bartók's opera *Bluebeard's Castle*.

2008   Presents his most ambitious exhibition to date at the de Young Museum, San Francisco. Returns to his alma mater with an exhibition at the RISD Museum of Art. Exhibits at the Desert Botanical Garden in Phoenix.

2009   Begins *Silvered* series. Mounts a garden exhibition at the Franklin Park Conservatory, Columbus, Ohio. Participates in the 53rd Venice Biennale with a *Mille Fiori* installation. Creates largest commission with multiple installations on the island resort of Sentosa, Singapore.

COLOPHON

This first printing of **CHIHULY CYLINDERS** is limited to 7,500 casebound copies. © 2010 Portland Press. All rights reserved. DVD is for private home viewing only.

Photography

Theresa Batty, Dick Busher, Jody Coleman, Gene Dwiggins, David Emery, George Erml, Ira Garber, Claire Garoutte, Warren Jagger, Uosis Juodvalkis, Russell Johnson, Scott M. Leen, Teresa Nouri Rishel, Terry Rishel, Roger Schreiber, William T. Schuck, Mike Seidl, Chuck Taylor, Robert Vinnedge, Charlie Wilkins

Designers

Ann Enomoto & Janná Giles

DVD Director

Peter West

Typeface

Frutiger

Printed and bound in China by Hing Yip Printing Co., Ltd.

Portland Press

Post Office Box 70856

Seattle, Washington 98127

800 574 7272

www.portlandpress.net

ISBN: 978-1-57684-177-8

Front cover:
Turquoise Green Soft Cylinder
with Ochre Drawing
1988, 17 x 17 x 14"

Pages 16–17:
Jerusalem Cylinder
in process
The Boathouse hotshop
Seattle, Washington, 1999